A TASTE OF

INDOCHINA

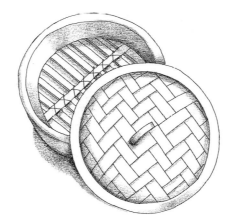

A TASTE OF
INDOCHINA

JAN CASTORINA & DIMITRA STAIS

PHOTOGRAPHY BY ASHLEY MACKEVICIUS

STYLING BY MARIE HELENE CLAUZON

ILLUSTRATIONS BY SUE NINHAM

BARRON'S

U.S. Edition Copyright © 1996 Barron's Educational Series, Inc.

Text Copyright © Jan Castorina & Dimitra Stais
Photography Copyright © Hodder Headline Australia Pty Ltd
First published in Australia in 1994 by Hodder & Stoughton
(Australia) Pty Limited
This United States edition is published by arrangement with
Hodder Headline Australia Pty Limited.

All inquiries should be addressed to:
Barron's Educational Series, Inc.
250 Wireless Boulevard,
Hauppauge, NY 11788-3917

ISBN 0-8120-6602-2

Library of Congress Card No. 96-302

Library of Congress Cataloging-in-Publication Data
Castorina, Jan.
    A taste of Indochina / Jan Castorina & Dimitra Stais ;
photography by Ashley Mackevicius ; styling by Marie Helene
Clauzon ; illustrations by Sue Ninham.
      p.   cm.
    Includes index.
    ISBN 0-8120-6602-2
    1. Cookery, Southeast Asian.   I. Stais, Dimitra.   II. Title.
TX724.5.S68C37   1996   96-302
641.5959—dc20   CIP

Printed in Hong Kong
987654321

Con

tents

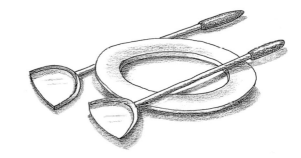

A Taste of Indochina

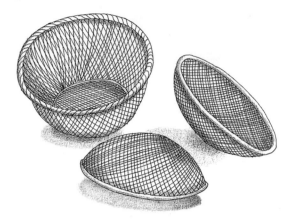

This book is an exploration of the flavors of Thailand, Vietnam, Laos and Cambodia.

The flavors of Thailand are varied and unique. In each region the food is prepared differently, sometimes subtly and sometimes quite remarkably.

In a Thai family meal there are several courses, all of which are usually served at one time. A curry, a soup and a large bowl of steamed jasmine or sticky rice are the main features and are often served with a salad dish and a noodle dish. The soup may be eaten before or after the rest of the meal.

Delicious sauces and condiments are served with the meal to add extra flavor and explosions of spice.

Vietnamese, Laotian and Cambodian dishes are distinctively light and delicate in flavor, with an abundant use of crisp raw vegetables to accompany every meal. What makes these foods so healthy is the many raw salads and vegetables they include. Most cooked dishes are either steamed or stir-fried using minimal oil.

A typical meal in this part of Asia will consist of a soup, a noodle dish, a meat dish, a bowl of glutinous or steamed rice, a platter of assorted vegetables and some fish sauce for dipping. There may be a separate bowl of chili sauce to add spice to the meal.

Desserts from these countries are usually based on fresh fruits and coconut and are served at more formal dinners. Sweets are often eaten as snacks during the day, however, as in Thailand, where they are bought from street vendors.

The Pantry Guide

In the following pages there is a description of some unusual ingredients and substitutes where possible. There are a few items you may not have heard of, but they are easily obtainable from Asian food stores and some supermarkets. Most of the sauces and pastes will last for many months; once you have them, they are always on hand to make delicious and simple dishes.

As these wonderful cuisines have become more and more popular, some thoughtful food manufacturers have gone to great lengths to make their ingredients a supermarket item. Ask at your favorite supermarket; you will be surprised what is available to you.

These are the essential ingredients that you will find described in detail within this pantry guide:

Bean Sauce
Chinese Dried Mushrooms
Coconut Cream
Coconut Milk
Curry Paste
Daikon Radish
Dried Shrimp
Egg Pastry
Fish Sauce
Green Papaya (pawpaw)
Noodles

Oil
Oyster Sauce
Palm Sugar (gula jawa)
Pickled Mustard
Rice
Rice Paper
Rice Vinegar
Sambal Oelek
Sesame Oil
Shrimp Paste
Soy Sauce

Split Yellow Mung Beans
Spring Roll Wrappers
Sugarcane
Sweet Chili Sauce
Tamarind
Taro
Tofu, Firm or Hard
   (bean curd)
Wonton Wrappers

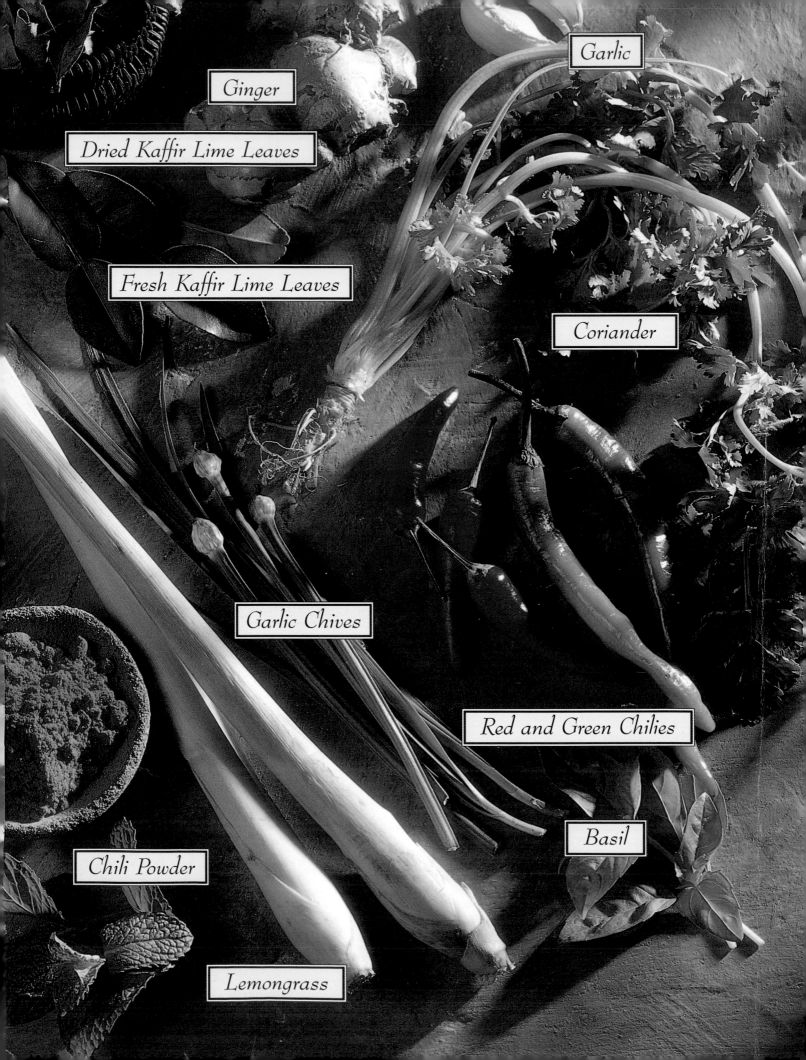

Garlic

Ginger

Dried Kaffir Lime Leaves

Fresh Kaffir Lime Leaves

Coriander

Garlic Chives

Red and Green Chilies

Basil

Chili Powder

Lemongrass

Bean Sauce

This is a thick sauce made from soybeans. If unavailable, substitute a little of the stronger-flavored black bean sauce.

Chinese Dried Mushrooms

These are found in Asian food stores and some supermarkets in plastic packets. Soak in hot water or stock for about 20 minutes until soft. The stem is removed, then the mushroom is sliced or left whole depending on the recipe. These have a strong flavor and are used sparingly. You can substitute fresh mushrooms but they do not have the same flavor.

Coconut Cream

Coconut cream is available from supermarkets and Asian food stores. It is usually canned or sold in small, sealed packets. Coconut milk can be used as a substitute, but it has a much thinner consistency.

Curry Paste

Use good quality purchased or homemade curry pastes in the recipes. You can buy excellent red and green curry pastes from supermarkets as well as in Asian food stores. Other varieties of curry paste can also be found in Asian food stores.

Daikon Radish

A long, thick, white, cylindrical vegetable that has a strong flavor.

This radish is often used fresh to add pungency and a lovely crisp texture to salads.

Dried Shrimp

Available in packets in Asian food stores. They have a strong fishy flavor and should be stored in the refrigerator, preferably in an airtight container.

Egg Pastry

Available refrigerated in Asian food stores. It is found in rounds and squares and can be frozen for up to two months; thaw in the refrigerator.

Fish Sauce

This is used throughout Southeast Asia. It is made from small fish or shrimp (prawns) that are fermented. The sauce adds a burst of flavor to many dishes, including sauces and condiments. It is found in supermarkets and Asian food stores.

Green Papaya (pawpaw)

This is the unripe red or yellow papaya, which is thinly sliced or grated and used in a salad. The skin should be a bright green color and the flesh pale, almost white. Ripe papaya cannot be used as a substitute.

Noodles

Bean Thread Vermicelli Noodles Use the noodles sold in 1.75 oz (50g) packets. They are opaque white when raw; after soaking in boiling water for 10 minutes they become translucent and soft.

Fresh Egg Noodles Found in the refrigerator in Asian food stores, these may be very thin or thick. They are also available in ribbons about $^1/_4$ in (4mm) wide. The noodles are made from wheat flour and egg and are used in a wide range of dishes. They are usually

boiled for several minutes before using.

Fresh Rice Noodles (banh pho) These are sold in sealed plastic packages near the counter or in the refrigerator in Asian food stores. They can be bought sliced or unsliced. The sliced version is in strips about $^1/_2$ in (1cm) wide. If you find the unsliced version, just cut slices from the block without unfolding it first. These noodles are soaked in boiling water for about 10 minutes before using.

Rice Stick Noodles These are long, thin strips about $^1/_4$ in (5mm) wide that must be soaked in boiling water for about 10 minutes. They are simple and easy to prepare and are found in supermarkets and Asian food stores.

Rice Vermicelli Noodles These are made from rice and water, like all the rice noodles, and are probably the most widely used noodles in Vietnam. They are readily available in most supermarkets. Soak in hot water and use in salads and stir-fries, or deep-fry. When deep-fried they puff and become crisp.

Somen Noodles These wheat-based noodles, very popular in Japanese cuisine, are also widely used by the Vietnamese. They are long, thin white noodles wrapped in bundles.

Wheat Noodles Sold fresh, these thick noodles are made from wheat and water.

Oil

Use a light-flavored oil in these recipes, such as safflower or canola. Extra light olive oil, which has virtually no flavor, can also be used.

Oyster Sauce

This dark brown sauce contains oyster extract. It adds a rich flavor and is used sparingly as it is quite salty. There is no substitute for this sauce.

Palm Sugar (gula jawa)

Made from the sap of the coconut palm, this has almost a caramel flavor. You will usually find it in cylinders or blocks, ready to be grated. It is very hard and compact, unlike white sugar. You can use brown sugar, but the dish will not have quite the same flavor.

Pickled Mustard

Made from green mustard cabbage, pickled mustard is the young and tender heart of the plant preserved or pickled in brine. It is sold at most Asian food stores in vacuum-sealed packets.

Rice

Jasmine rice, glutinous rice, and long-grain rice are most commonly used. They are found in super-markets and Asian food stores.

Rice Paper

This is used for making fresh spring rolls. You can find it in Asian food stores. Soak the rice paper in warm water until just soft before using.

Rice Vinegar

Milder and less sour than other vinegars, rice vinegar has a delicate sweetness.

Sambal Oelek

Sambal oelek is a paste made from red chilies, vinegar and salt. It is not a traditional ingredient but is used often throughout this book simply because it adds a delicious flavor and color. It is found in supermarkets and Asian food stores.

Sesame Oil

Made from toasted sesame seeds, this has a smoky flavor and is added to stir-fries and other dishes in small quantities—a little goes a long way. It is not usually used for frying.

Shrimp Paste

This paste is very strong smelling but adds a delicious flavor to many dishes. The paste must be cooked first, then used in the recipe. Don't let the odor put you off, as shrimp paste is quite subtle in the finished recipe.

Soy Sauce

Use a light soy sauce from Asian food stores or supermarkets. It is made from fermented soybeans.

Split Yellow Mung Beans

These dried yellow beans are sold in packets in most Asian food stores. They do not require soaking.

Spring Roll Wrappers

These can be found in supermarkets and Asian food stores and come in several sizes. For best results, use the size called for in the recipe. There is no substitute.

Sugarcane

Fresh sugarcane can be found in Asian, Indian and Caribbean food stores, but the cane is more readily available in cans. Fresh sugarcane needs to be peeled first, but the canned product is ready to use.

Sweet Chili Sauce

This is a spicy but sweet sauce that goes with all types of Thai food from appetizers to noodles. It is found in supermarkets and Asian food stores. A must for the pantry.

Tamarind

Available as a purée or concentrate, tamarind has a tart flavor. Use half the amount of concentrate as puree. Use vinegar or lemon juice as a substitute.

Taro

Taro root is an oval-shaped tuber with a hairy brown skin. It is creamy and smooth like a potato; sweet potato can be substituted.

Tofu, Firm or Hard (bean curd)

Many people prefer the tofu sold in Asian food stores or health food stores. The firmer the tofu, the better it is for stir-frying or panfrying. Made from soybeans, tofu is an excellent source of protein. It marinates well, soaking in all the flavors around it. Keep leftover tofu in a deep dish covered with water for up to a few days, changing the water daily.

Wonton Wrappers

These are available in rounds or squares roughly 3 in (8cm) wide. You will find them refrigerated in Asian food stores.

Appetizers and Snacks

I n Thailand, appetizers are not usually eaten before a main meal. Instead, appetizers and snacks are eaten during the day, purchased from the many street food vendors selling tasty morsels. A large variety of foods from Vietnam, Laos and Cambodia is suitable for serving as appetizers, as many dishes are made in small packages or in small portions.

The appetizers and snacks in the following pages can be served at cocktail parties, as the first course of an Asian meal or for most entertaining situations. Delicious dipping sauces are often served with them, adding an extra dimension to the exotic flavors.

RIGHT: Belgian Endive with Chili Pork

Belgian Endive with Chili Pork

This is a stylish appetizer for entertaining. For a more casual appearance, serve with squares of raw vegetables, such as peppers, or fill small fresh mushrooms with the mixture. The chili pork can be made several hours ahead and warmed before serving.

1 tablespoon oil
2 cloves garlic, crushed
1 tablespoon finely chopped fresh ginger
4 green onions, finely chopped
1/2 teaspoon shrimp paste
1 tablespoon chopped lemongrass
2 teaspoons sambal oelek
5oz (150g) pork fillet, finely chopped
8oz 250g) cherry tomatoes, quartered
1 tablespoon coconut cream
3 tablespoons chopped fresh coriander
1 Belgian endive

Heat oil in frying pan and add garlic, ginger, green onions, shrimp paste, lemongrass and sambal oelek. Cook mixture, stirring, until the green onion is soft.

Add pork and cook, stirring until it just begins to turn white. Stir in tomatoes and coconut cream and bring to a boil. Simmer the mixture uncovered until mixture thickens and tomatoes are well cooked. Stir in coriander.

While mixture is simmering, carefully separate the Belgian endive leaves, wash and drain well. Spoon chili pork mixture onto individual endive leaves just before serving.

SERVES 4

Sesame Shrimp Toasts

This appetizer is simple to prepare and can be made several hours ahead. Assemble and broil the toasts just before serving. They go wonderfully with predinner drinks or at an afternoon get-together.

4 thick slices bread
1 tablespoon oil
2oz (60g) ground pork
8 uncooked large shrimp, peeled, deveined and chopped
1 large clove garlic, crushed
1 egg white
2 tablespoons sesame seeds
2 tablespoons chopped fresh coriander
1/4 teaspoon chili powder
ground black pepper

Cut bread into 2in (5cm) rounds using cookie cutter. You should be able to cut 3 rounds from each slice. Toast rounds lightly on both sides under hot broiler.

Heat oil in frying pan, add pork and cook, stirring, until just cooked. Add shrimp and garlic and stir until shrimp are just pink; cool. Combine pork mixture with egg white, sesame seeds, coriander, chili powder and pepper in bowl.

Spoon pork mixture onto toast rounds, pressing lightly and forming a mound on each one. Arrange toasts on baking sheet and broil until heated through and crisp and browned on top. Serve hot.

MAKES ABOUT 12

Pork and Crab Cubes

The cubes can be made a day ahead and served cold, or cooked an hour or so ahead and served warm.

5¹/₂oz (170g) can crabmeat, drained and flaked
1 single chicken breast fillet, very finely chopped
5oz (150g) lean ground pork
4 green onions, finely chopped
2 tablespoons chopped fresh coriander
1 egg, lightly beaten
1 tablespoon coconut cream
1 tablespoon sweet chili sauce
extra coriander leaves

Combine all ingredients except extra coriander leaves in bowl and mix well. Spoon into foil-lined 3in x 10in (8cm x 26cm) cake pan, pressing firmly. Cover pan tightly with foil.

Place pan in bamboo steamer over a wok one-quarter filled with boiling water. Cover steamer and cook over gently boiling water 30 minutes.

Remove pan from steamer, remove foil, and drain away any excess liquid in pan. Let loaf stand for 40 minutes.

Turn loaf onto work surface and cut into 1¹/₂in (4cm) cubes. Top each cube with an extra coriander leaf and pierce with toothpick before serving.

MAKES ABOUT 12

~ Tip ~

You can also steam food in a double boiler or a saucepan steamer. If you don't have either, place the food on a rack over a baking dish half filled with boiling water. Cover the whole thing with foil and bake in a 350°F (180°C) oven for the required time. Check that the food is cooked before turning off the oven, as this method may take a little longer than stovetop steaming.

Panfried Fish Cakes

This is a very simple method of making delicious Thai-flavored fish cakes. They can be made in the size suggested, or you can make them smaller to serve at cocktail parties.

13oz (400g) boneless fish fillets
2 teaspoons purchased or homemade
  red curry paste
1 egg
4 green onions, chopped
1 teaspoon grated lime zest
2 tablespoons chopped fresh coriander
1 tablespoon oil

Grind fish, curry paste, and egg in processor until finely chopped. Blend in green onions, lime zest and coriander. Wet hands slightly and shape 2 tablespoons of mixture into a patty. Repeat with remaining mixture.

Heat oil in nonstick frying pan, add fish cakes, and cook until lightly browned underneath, then turn and cook other side until cooked through. Serve with Chili and Peanut Sauce (see THE ESSENTIALS).

MAKES ABOUT 10

Steamed Spicy Vegetarian Buns

1 envelope dry yeast
½ cup (4fl oz/125ml) warm water
¼ cup (2oz/60g) sugar
1 cup (5oz/150g) all-purpose flour
½ cup (2½oz/75g) self-rising flour
1 tablespoon butter, melted
FILLING
1 Chinese dried mushroom
1½oz (50g) firm tofu
2 teaspoons sesame oil
½ small leek, finely chopped
2 cloves garlic, crushed
1 teaspoon grated fresh ginger
1 tablespoon lime juice
½ small carrot, grated
1 tablespoon roasted unsalted cashews, chopped
2 teaspoons sweet chili sauce
1 tablespoon chopped fresh mint
2 teaspoons bean sauce
1 tablespoon tomato paste

Combine yeast, 2 tablespoons of the warm water, 1 teaspoon of the sugar, and 1 teaspoon of the all-purpose flour in small bowl. Cover and let stand in a warm place for about 15 minutes or until frothy. Sift remaining flours into large bowl, add remaining sugar, and mix well. Stir in yeast mixture, remaining water and butter and mix to form soft dough. Knead on floured surface until smooth and elastic, about 3 minutes. Place in lightly oiled bowl, cover with greased plastic wrap, and let stand in a warm place until doubled, about 1 hour.

Meanwhile, prepare filling. Cover mushroom with hot water in small bowl and let stand 30 minutes; drain. Finely chop mushroom, discarding stem. Cut tofu into ¼in (5mm) cubes. Heat sesame oil in frying pan. Add leek, garlic and ginger and cook until soft,

about 3 minutes. Let cool. Stir in mushroom, tofu, lime juice, carrot, cashews, chili sauce, mint, bean sauce and tomato paste.

Knead dough on floured surface for 5 minutes. Divide into 16 portions. Roll each portion into ball, then flatten into large round. Spoon 2 level teaspoons of filling onto center of each round. Gather edges to enclose filling, then pinch top to seal and form round bun.

Lightly brush 16 3½in (9cm) squares of waxed paper with sesame oil. Top each with bun, pinched side up, and arrange in large bamboo steamer. Steam until buns are dry to touch, about 8 minutes. (If your steamer is small, steam in 2 batches.) Serve warm.

MAKES 16

Shrimp with Leeks in Fish Sauce

8 medium uncooked shrimp
¼ teaspoon freshly ground black pepper
3 cloves garlic, crushed
2 tablespoons oil
1 leek, sliced
1½ tablespoons fish sauce
2 tablespoons lime juice
1 tablespoon chopped fresh garlic chives

Peel and devein the shrimp, leaving tails intact. Combine shrimp with pepper and half the garlic.

Heat half of oil in wok or frying pan. Add leek and remaining garlic and stir-fry until leek is just soft, about 2 minutes. Divide leek between serving plates and keep warm while preparing shrimp.

Heat remaining oil in same wok over high heat. Add shrimp mixture and stir-fry until shrimp are just cooked, about 3 minutes. Stir in fish sauce and lime juice. Serve shrimp on leeks, drizzled with pan juices, and sprinkled with chives.

SERVES 2

LEFT: From top: Steamed Spicy Vegetarian Buns; Shrimp with Leeks in Fish Sauce

Chicken and Coriander Rounds

The rounds can be made a day ahead.

2 tablespoons oil
2 teaspoons purchased or homemade green
curry paste
1 clove garlic, crushed
1 small onion, chopped
¹/₂ small red bell pepper, finely chopped
10oz (300g) chicken thigh fillets, chopped
1 egg, lightly beaten
FILLING
1 cup (1oz/30g) fresh coriander leaves
¹/₂ cup (¹/₂oz/15g) chopped garlic chives
1 teaspoon purchased or homemade green
curry paste

Heat oil in frying pan over low heat. Add curry paste, garlic, onion and bell pepper and cook until onion is very soft, about 5 minutes. Cool.

Blend chicken with onion mixture and egg to paste consistency in food processor.

For filling, combine all filling ingredients with 2 tablespoons processed chicken mixture in food processor and blend until well chopped.

Divide chicken mixture into 6 even portions. Spread 1 portion on 10 in (25cm) square of parchment paper into a 4¹/₂in (12cm) square. Spoon one-third of filling mixture along center of chicken mixture.

Spoon another portion of chicken mixture over top of filling and spread to cover filling. Roll up firmly in the paper, shaping into sausage, and twist ends of the paper to seal. Repeat with remaining chicken mixture and filling. Arrange rolls in bamboo steamer and place in wok one-quarter filled with boiling water. Steam rolls over gently boiling water 20 minutes.

Remove rolls from wok, loosen paper and drain away any liquid. Let stand for 15 minutes before cutting diagonally into slices ¹/₂in (1cm) thick. Can be served warm or cold.

MAKES ABOUT 30

Spread chicken mixture over filling.

Roll up firmly and twist ends of paper to seal.

RIGHT: Chicken and Coriander Rounds

Garlic Herb Oysters

This aromatic mix of herbs makes the oysters taste delicious, especially when cooked in butter, but they must be eaten warm. If you are planning to serve them cold, cook the oysters in 2 teaspoons oil instead of the butter.

12 fresh oysters in half shells
1 tablespoon butter
2 teaspoons fish sauce
1 clove garlic, crushed
1 small red chili, seeded and finely chopped
1 teaspoon grated fresh ginger
1 teaspoon finely chopped lemongrass
1 teaspoon chopped fresh mint
2 teaspoons lime juice

Remove oysters from shells; reserve shells. Heat butter and fish sauce in small frying pan. Add garlic, chili, ginger and lemongrass and cook, stirring, until the mixture begins to foam, about 1 minute. Add oysters and toss until well coated and heated through.

Place oysters back in their shells, sprinkle with mint, and drizzle with lime juice.

SERVES 2

Beef Omelet Scrolls

These attractive little appetizers are best eaten warm. They can be made up to 4 hours ahead and reheated.

2 eggs
2 tablespoons all-purpose flour
2 teaspoons chopped fresh garlic chives
1 tablespoon milk
3 teaspoons fish sauce
1 tablespoon oil
1½ tablespoons coconut cream
8 fresh mint leaves
BEEF FILLING
11oz (350g) beef fillet or round steak
1 tablespoon fish sauce
2 cloves garlic, crushed
2 tablespoons lemon juice
1 teaspoon sesame oil
2 teaspoons oil
1 teaspoon grated lemon zest
2 tablespoons roasted unsalted cashews
*   finely chopped*

Beat eggs, flour, garlic chives, milk and 2 teaspoons fish sauce in bowl until smooth. Heat half of oil in 9in (23cm) omelet pan. Pour in half the egg mixture and swirl pan so mixture covers bottom. Cook gently until set. Slide omelet onto a board, then cut into quarters. Repeat with remaining mixture.

To make filling, cut beef into strips ⅛in (3mm) thick. Combine beef, fish sauce, garlic and lemon juice in medium bowl. Cover and refrigerate at least 1 hour or overnight.

Heat oils in medium frying pan. Add beef mixture, and stir-fry until beef is just cooked. Transfer to bowl, add zest and cashews, and mix well.

Spread each omelet quarter with some combined coconut cream and extra fish sauce. Place some beef strips along center, top with mint leaf. Fold over corners, then secure with toothpicks and serve.

MAKES 8

Fresh Chicken and Crab Spring Rolls

These spring rolls cannot be made too far ahead because the rice paper dries out quickly. Most of your time is spent on the fillings, so have them and dipping sauce all prepared ahead, then make the spring rolls close to serving time.

1 teaspoon honey
¼ teaspoon chili powder
1 tablespoon rice vinegar
1 single chicken breast fillet
2 teaspoons fish sauce
2oz (60g) rice vermicelli noodles
3 Chinese dried mushrooms
½ cup (1½oz/40g) bean sprouts
1 small carrot, grated
3 green onions, chopped
2 pickled cucumbers or gherkins, thinly sliced
2 leaves butter or iceberg lettuce, finely shredded
2½oz (75g) cooked crabmeat
¼ cup (¼oz/7g) fresh coriander sprigs
½ cup (½oz/15g) fresh mint leaves
12 6½in (16cm) rounds of rice paper
Fish Dipping Sauce (page 155)
2 teaspoons roasted unsalted peanuts, finely chopped

Combine honey, chili powder and vinegar in bowl, add chicken and stir until chicken is well coated. Cover and refrigerate at least 1 hour or overnight.

Broil chicken until cooked through; cool. Slice thinly, then drizzle with fish sauce.

Place vermicelli in heatproof bowl and cover with boiling water. Let stand for 30 minutes, then drain. Using scissors, cut vermicelli into shorter lengths.

Place mushrooms in bowl and cover with hot water. Let stand for 30 minutes; drain. Slice mushrooms thinly, discarding tough stems.

Arrange fillings on work surface in order of use: first chicken, then vermicelli, mushrooms, bean sprouts, carrot, green onions, pickles, lettuce, crabmeat, coriander and mint. Have bowl of warm water nearby large enough for the rice paper.

Soak a sheet of rice paper in water until pliable, about 20 seconds, then place on board. Place some of each filling on base end of rice paper and roll up firmly but carefully, folding in sides. Work quickly to keep rice paper from drying out. Repeat with remaining rice paper and fillings. Place on a serving plate and serve immediately or cover with plastic wrap and refrigerate up to 3 hours.

Serve rolls with fish dipping sauce sprinkled with peanuts.

MAKES 12

~ Tip ~

To make your own chili powder, grind dried chilies to powder in coffee grinder, blender, or mortar with pestle. Store in clean jar.

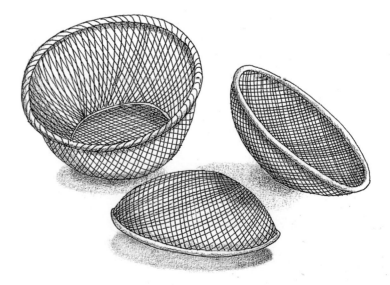

Wooden bowl from Corso del Fiori

Skewered Saté Shrimp

The shrimp can be prepared a day ahead and then quickly broiled or barbecued just before serving. This is a very popular appetizer and it's not too spicy.

12 uncooked jumbo shrimp
1 clove garlic, crushed
1 tablespoon peanut butter
2 tablespoons very finely chopped onion
2 teaspoons fish sauce
1/2 cup (4fl oz/125ml) coconut cream
1/4 teaspoon chili powder (more if preferred)
1/2 teaspoon ground turmeric

Peel shrimp, leaving tails intact. Place shrimp on ends of short bamboo skewers, skewering through end and just above tail of each shrimp. Place shrimp in a dish or pitcher keeping skewer ends out of the dish.

Combine all remaining ingredients in bowl and pour over shrimp making sure they are well coated. Cover shrimp and refrigerate at least several hours or overnight to allow flavors to develop.

Broil or barbecue satés, turning and brushing with any remaining marinade, until just cooked through. Serve immediately.

SERVES 3 TO 4

Lime and Pork Patties

Make this mixture a day ahead, shape into patties, and cook just before serving. The lime flavor gives the patties a zesty tang.

8oz (250g) lean ground pork
2 cloves garlic, crushed
1 teaspoon grated lime zest
1 tablespoon fish sauce
2 teaspoons oyster sauce
2 teaspoons sambal oelek
1/4 cup (1/2oz/15g) finely chopped green onions
1 egg white
1 tablespoon oil
Chili Lime Sauce (page 154)

Combine all ingredients except oil in bowl and mix well. Shape tablespoons of mixture into little patties.

Heat oil in frying pan, add patties in single layer and cook until lightly browned underneath. Turn patties and cook other side until browned and just cooked through; don't overcook or the patties will become dry.

Serve the patties with chili lime sauce.

MAKES ABOUT 15

*LEFT: From top: Skewered Saté
Shrimp; Lime and Pork Patties*

Chicken and Corn Wedges

Baking makes a healthy alternative to frying and there is no last-minute cooking to do—you can pop this in the oven while preparing other dishes.

3 eggs
9oz (270g) can corn kernels
2½ tablespoons all-purpose flour, sifted
1 cup (7oz/200g) finely chopped
  cooked chicken
½ teaspoon grated lime zest
1 medium-sized red chili, finely chopped
1 tablespoon chopped fresh mint
1 tablespoon chopped fresh coriander
2 teaspoons fish sauce
sweet chili sauce

Combine all ingredients in bowl and mix well. Spoon mixture into greased 7in (18cm) round cake pan. Bake in 325°F (160°C) oven until cooked through, about 20 minutes.

Cool 10 minutes, then turn out onto board and cut into wedges. Serve with sweet chili sauce.

MAKES ABOUT 12 WEDGES

Crisp Cashew Bags

This is a simpler version of the deep-fried pouches often seen in Thai restaurants. The baking eliminates messy deep frying and extra oil.

1 clove garlic, crushed
½ cup (2½oz/80oz) raw cashews
½ cup (2½oz/80g) finely grated carrot
2 tablespoons sesame seeds, toasted
¼ cup (¼oz/7g) finely chopped garlic chives
1 teaspoon fish sauce
1 tablespoon chopped fresh coriander
2 tablespoons oil
20 3in (8cm) square egg pastry sheets
1 teaspoon cornstarch
1 tablespoon water
bottled Thai sweet chili sauce

Combine garlic, cashews, carrot, sesame seeds, garlic chives, fish sauce, coriander and 1 tablespoon oil in food processor and chop finely.

Spoon 2 teaspoons of mixture onto pastry sheet. Combine cornstarch and water and brush over edges of pastry. Gather edges of pastry sheet around filling and pinch firmly to form a little bag.

Brush bag lightly with some of remaining oil and place on lightly greased baking sheet. Repeat with remaining filling and pastry. Bake in 400°F (200°C) oven until lightly browned all over, about 10 minutes. Serve with bottled Thai sweet chili sauce.

MAKES 20

~ Tip ~
To toast sesame seeds, place them in a pan and stir constantly over medium heat until lightly browned. Remove the seeds from pan to cool.

Oven-Baked Spring Rolls

1¹/₂oz (50g) bean thread vermicelli noodles
1 tablespoon oil
4oz (125g) lean ground pork
8 uncooked large shrimp, peeled, deveined, and
    finely chopped
1 large clove garlic, chopped
2 coriander roots, finely chopped
4 green onions, finely chopped
1in (2.5cm) piece fresh ginger, finely shredded
1 teaspoon sambal oelek
2 tablespoons chopped fresh coriander
26 spring roll wrappers
1 tablespoon cornstarch
1 tablespoon water
oil
sweet chili sauce or Chili and Peanut
    Sauce (page 154)

Place noodles in heatproof bowl. Cover with hot water, and soak 10 minutes. Drain noodles and cut into 2in (5cm) lengths.

Heat oil in frying pan. Add pork, shrimp, garlic, coriander roots, green onions, ginger and sambal oelek and cook, stirring, until shrimp are just cooked; cool. Stir in noodles and coriander and mix well.

Place a tablespoon of noodle mixture onto spring roll wrapper. Combine cornstarch and water and brush over edges of wrapper. Fold in sides and roll up firmly. Place seam side down on oiled baking sheet and brush lightly with oil.

Repeat with the remaining filling and spring roll wrappers. Bake the rolls in a 400°F (200°C) oven until lightly browned and crisp, about 20 minutes.

Serve with bottled Thai sweet chili sauce or Chili and Peanut Sauce.

MAKES 26

Lemongrass Mussels

You can prepare these mussels several hours ahead and cook them just before serving. Smaller mussels are delicious in this recipe and are a nice size for appetizers.

20 small black mussels
1 single chicken breast fillet, chopped
2 teaspoons purchased or homemade green
    curry paste
¹/₂ small onion, finely chopped
¹/₂ small carrot, finely grated
1¹/₂ tablespoons chopped lemongrass
lemon juice
Chopped fresh coriander

Scrub mussels and debeard by pulling away fibrous bits protruding from between shell halves.

Place mussels in large pan with a little water. Cover and bring to boil. Remove mussels from the pan as they open; cool. Discard any mussels that do not open. Remove one half shell from each mussel and discard. Loosen mussel meat in remaining half shells.

Combine all remaining ingredients in food processor and blend until finely chopped. Spoon onto mussels, shaping around mussel meat.

Broil mussels until lightly browned and topping is cooked through. Serve topped with a squeeze of lemon juice and chopped coriander.

MAKES 20

Barbecued Shrimp on Sugarcane

These unusual appetizers are one of the delights of Vietnamese cuisine. When the sugarcane sticks are barbecued, the ends will char and have a delicious raw sweetness once you eat through the shrimp mixture and start chewing on the cane. If you cannot find sugarcane, use stalks of fresh lemongrass instead.

20oz (600g) medium uncooked shrimp
4 cloves garlic, crushed
4 green onions, chopped
2 teaspoons sugar
2 teaspoons fish sauce
2 teaspoons cornstarch
1 slice bacon, finely chopped
5 5¹/2in (14cm) sticks canned sugarcane
Fish Dipping Sauce (page 155)
2 teaspoons roasted unsalted peanuts,
  chopped

Peel and devein shrimp. Combine shrimp, garlic, green onions, sugar, fish sauce, cornstarch and bacon in food processor and blend until smooth and pasty. Cut sugarcane sticks in half lengthwise. With lightly oiled hands, mold level tablespoons of shrimp mixture around the center of the sugarcane sticks.

Heat greased barbecue hotplate, griddle or broiler until hot. Cook until shrimp mixture is cooked through, turning occasionally.

Serve with a small bowl of fish dipping sauce. Sprinkle with chopped peanuts.

MAKES ABOUT 10

Process shrimp mixture until smooth and pasty.

Mold level tablespoons of shrimp mixture around the sugarcane sticks.

RIGHT: Barbecued Shrimp on Sugarcane

Sesame Lamb and Baby Onion Sticks

This is equally delicious made with beef fillet.

11oz (350g) lamb fillet
1 clove garlic, crushed
1 teaspoon grated fresh ginger
1 tablespoon lime juice
¼ teaspoon paprika
4 teaspoons chopped fresh coriander
1½ tablespoons fish sauce
4 small brown pickling onions, halved
Peanut Sauce (see page 155)
5 teaspoons sesame seeds, toasted
2 teaspoons sesame oil

Cut lamb into 1¼in (3cm) pieces. Combine lamb, garlic, ginger, lime juice, paprika, 2 teaspoons coriander, fish sauce and onions in bowl. Cover and refrigerate at least 1 hour or overnight, stirring occasionally.

Drain lamb and onions, reserving marinade. Divide lamb and onion pieces into 8 portions and thread onto bamboo skewers. Grill or barbecue until lamb is just cooked, turning once during cooking.

While lamb sticks are cooking, prepare dipping sauce by combining peanut sauce with 2 tablespoons sesame seeds and sesame oil in small bowl. Serve sticks sprinkled with remaining sesame seeds and coriander and accompanied by dipping sauce.

MAKES 8

~ *Tip* ~
To avoid burning bamboo skewers during cooking, soak in water for about 1 hour before using.

Oven-Baked Marinated Pork Fillet

A healthier alternative to pork spareribs, pork fillet is low in fat and very tender. This baked pork fillet can be used instead of purchased barbecued pork in any recipe. Eat it hot or cold, served in thin slices as an appetizer with some fish dipping sauce. If you prefer to use pork spareribs, you will need about 1¼lbs (600g) of spare ribs.

2 tablespoons sugar
1 tablespoon fish sauce
2 cloves garlic, crushed
1 tablespoon chopped lemongrass
½ teaspoon five spice powder
½ teaspoon dried chili flakes
2 teaspoons rice vinegar
1 tablespoon chopped fresh mint
1 tablespoon tomato paste
1 clove garlic
10oz (300g) pork fillet

Using mortar and pestle or blender, blend sugar, fish sauce, crushed garlic, lemongrass, five spice powder chili flakes, vinegar, mint and tomato paste until smooth.

Cut extra garlic clove into 6 thin strips. Make 6 small incisions in pork fillet and insert garlic strips. Brush marinade mixture all over pork. Cover and refrigerate at least 2 hours or overnight to allow flavors to develop.

Place pork on wire rack in roasting pan and add a little water to pan to prevent juices from burning. Bake in a 400°F (200°C) oven until just cooked through, about 40 minutes. Cool slightly before slicing.

SERVES 4 TO 6

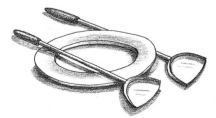

Curried Pork Turnovers

Taro is becoming more available when in season, but if you cannot find any, substitute white sweet potato, which will give the dough a delicate sweetness.

8oz (250g) taro, peeled and chopped
2 tablespoons butter, chopped
¼ cup (1½oz/40g) all-purpose flour
1 tablespoon black sesame seeds or toasted white sesame seeds
Shallot Oil (see page 155)
FILLING
4oz (125g) ground pork
2 teaspoons finely chopped garlic chives
1 teaspoon fish sauce
2 teaspoons oil
1 tablespoon finely chopped lemongrass
1 small onion, finely chopped
2 teaspoons curry powder
2 teaspoons chopped fresh coriander

Boil or steam taro until tender, about 10 minutes. Mash with butter until completely smooth; let cool. Combine mashed taro with flour and sesame seeds in bowl.

To make filling, combine pork, garlic chives and fish sauce in bowl. Cover and refrigerate 1 hour. Heat oil in wok or frying pan. Add lemongrass, onion, curry powder and coriander and cook 1 minute or until aromatic. Add pork mixture and cook over high heat, breaking up lumps, until meat is dry and has changed color. Cool.

Divide taro dough into 12 portions. Flatten each portion into a 3in (8cm) round on lightly floured surface, using floured palm of your hand.

Spoon 2 level teaspoons filling onto center of each dough round. Fold over to enclose filling, pinching edges or pressing with fork to seal.

Arrange turnovers on lightly greased baking sheet and brush with shallot oil. Bake in a 400°F (200°C) oven 10 minutes. Turn turnovers, brush with more oil and bake 8 more minutes or until well browned.

MAKES 12

Tomato Dip with Vegetable Crudités

This dip is ideal for dieters. It contains no added fat and is a wonderful blend of flavors cooked down to a spicy dip. It can be made up to 3 days ahead. Use any vegetables for crudités.

5 small ripe tomatoes
3 cloves garlic
2 small red onions, finely chopped
2 teaspoons chopped fresh coriander root
1 long green chili, finely chopped
1 teaspoon tomato paste
1 teaspoon fish sauce
1 tablespoon chopped fresh coriander
1½oz (50g) okra
3½oz (100g) cauliflower or broccoli, cut into small florets
1oz (30g) snow peas
1 small red or green bell pepper, cut into thick strips

Cut large cross in base end of each tomato, just cutting through skin. Add tomatoes to pan of boiling water and after water returns to boil, boil for 1 minute. Drain and rinse under cold water. Peel away skin.

Bruise garlic by flattening with flat side of knife, then chop coarsely. Combine garlic, onion, coriander root and chili in a wok or medium saucepan and cook, stirring constantly to avoid burning, 1 minute or until aromatic. Stir in tomatoes and simmer uncovered until thick, about 8 minutes, stirring occasionally. Add tomato paste and fish sauce and mix well.

Spoon dip into serving bowl, sprinkle with coriander and serve with crudités.

MAKES ABOUT ¾ CUP

Flavour-Filled Soups

Most of the Vietnamese, Laotian and Cambodian soups are based on a beautifully light stock with an abundance of vegetables, noodles and fish, eggs or meats (such as chicken, beef, pork and duck) to make them a hearty meal in themselves.

In the Thai soups, the blend of sour, spicy and citrus flavours or the creamy coconut flavours makes for a scrumptious beginning to a meal or eaten as just a meal by themselves.

Use either home-made stock or buy good quality ready-made stock, concentrate or cubes. Some of the soups will serve four as an entrée or two quite amply.

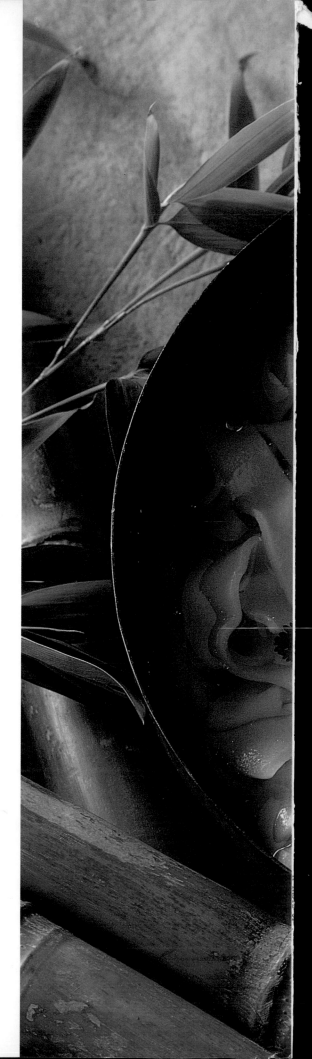

RIGHT: Chicken and Rice Noodle Soup

Chicken and Rice Noodle Soup

This soup is traditionally made with beef and is quite often served for breakfast. I make it with chicken and find it makes a great lunch or dinner. Have some lime wedges and mild chili sauce on the table for flavoring the soup.

1 single chicken breast fillet
1in (2.5cm) piece fresh ginger
3 cups (24fl oz/750ml) well-flavored chicken stock
1 star anise
1in (2.5cm) cinnamon stick
1 small onion, chopped
1 tablespoon fish sauce
8oz (250g) fresh rice noodles (banh pho)
2 small red chilies, finely sliced
2 green onions, finely sliced
1 tablespoon fresh coriander leaves
1 tablespoon small fresh mint leaves

Cut chicken into ⅛in (3mm) slices. Peel ginger and cut into very fine julienne. Combine stock with half of ginger, star anise, cinnamon, onion and fish sauce in saucepan and bring to boil. Reduce heat and simmer, covered, 10 minutes. Strain stock, discarding solids.

Return stock to pan and bring to simmer. Add chicken and simmer until chicken is just cooked, about 5 minutes. Meanwhile, place noodles in heatproof bowl, cover with boiling water and let stand. Drain noodles, place in soup bowls and top with soup. Serve soup sprinkled with chilies, green onions, coriander and mint.

SERVES 2

VARIATION
This soup can be made with beef stock and thinly sliced beef fillet for traditional flavor.

Lemon and Dill Seafood Soup

Use lemon leaves that are chemical free, or if unavailable, double the lemongrass. Be sure to crease the leaves along the center vein to release their aroma during cooking.

1 Chinese dried mushroom
7 oz (200g) lingcod fillets
4 large uncooked shrimp, peeled and deveined
2 teaspoons fish sauce
½ teaspoon freshly ground black pepper
2 cloves garlic, sliced
3 green onions, sliced
2 fresh lemon leaves
1 tablespoon chopped fresh lemongrass
1 tablespoon tamarind purée
3 cups (24fl oz/750ml) fish stock or water
1 small tomato, peeled, seeded and finely chopped
1 tablespoon chopped fresh dill
1 small red chili, finely chopped
½ cup (1½oz/40g) bean sprouts

Soak mushroom in hot water for 30 minutes; drain. Remove stem and cut mushroom into quarters. Cut lingcod into 1in (2.5cm) pieces. Combine lingcod, shrimp, fish sauce and pepper in bowl, cover and refrigerate 30 minutes.

Combine garlic, green onions, lemon leaves, lemongrass and tamarind in wok or frying pan and stir over heat about 1 minute or until aromatic. Add stock and tomato and bring to boil. Add mushroom and fish mixture and simmer uncovered until seafood is tender, about 2 minutes. Discard lemon leaves. Stir in dill and chili.

Divide bean sprouts among soup bowls, ladle hot soup over sprouts and serve immediately.

SERVES 4 AS AN ENTREE OR
2 AS A MAIN COURSE

Tomato and Egg Thread Soup

The tamarind puree gives this vegetarian soup its tangy flavor. You can use any vegetables available, such as broccoli or green beans, instead of the pumpkin, cauliflower and snow peas.

$3^{1}/2$oz (100g) pumpkin or rutabaga
$2^{1}/2$oz (75g) cauliflower
$1^{1}/2$oz (50g) snow peas
2 teaspoons oil
2 teaspoons chopped fresh coriander root
$1^{1}/2$ teaspoons galangal powder
2 teaspoons fish sauce
1 ripe tomato, peeled and chopped
1 cup (8fl oz/250ml) well-flavored vegetable stock
1 cup (8fl oz/250ml) water
2 teaspoons tamarind puree
2 teaspoons lime juice
2 green onions, sliced diagonally
2 tablespoons chopped fresh coriander
1 egg, lightly beaten
1 tablespoon fresh coriander leaves

Cut pumpkin into $^3/4$in (2cm) cubes. Cut cauliflower into small florets. Cut snow peas diagonally into strips $^1/2$in (1cm) wide.

Heat oil in wok or frying pan. Add coriander root, galangal, fish sauce and tomato and stir-fry about 1 minute or until aromatic. Add stock, water and tamarind puree and bring to boil. Add pumpkin and cauliflower and simmer uncovered 4 minutes. Add snow peas, lime juice, green onions and coriander and bring to boil. While boiling, pour in egg in thin stream, stirring constantly to form threads. Garnish with extra coriander leaves and serve.

SERVES 2

Aromatic Beef and Aniseed Soup

Ideal for a cold winter's dinner, this soup is best made a day ahead to allow the spice flavors to develop. Make the soup without adding the vegetables, then just before serving, bring to boil and add the zucchini, carrot, bean sauce and lime juice. Serve this with crusty rolls.

10oz (300g) beef blade steak
$^1/2$ small zucchini
$^1/2$ small carrot
1 tablespoon oil
1 clove garlic, crushed
1 onion, finely chopped
2 medium-sized ripe tomatoes, peeled and chopped
$1^1/2$in (3cm) piece fresh ginger, julienned
3 pieces star anise
1 tablespoon chopped lemongrass
3 cups (24fl oz/750ml) water
2 teaspoons bean sauce
1 tablespoon lime juice

Trim all fat from beef and slice beef into strips $^1/8$in (3mm) thick. Cut zucchini and carrot into thin strips $1^1/2$in (3cm) long.

Heat oil in wok or saucepan and brown beef in 2 batches; drain on paper towels. Add garlic and onion to wok and stir over heat until soft. Add tomatoes, ginger, star anise and lemongrass and stir over heat about 2 minutes or until aromatic. Return beef to wok. Add water and bring to boil, then simmer, covered, about 1 hour or until beef is tender. Add zucchini, carrot, bean sauce and lime juice and simmer for 1 minute. Serve immediately.

MAKES 2 LARGE SERVINGS

Thai-Style Shrimp Wonton Soup

If you prefer, you can buy ready-made wontons from the freezer section in Asian
food stores. There are also ready-made fish stocks available from supermarkets.

WONTONS

1lb (450g) uncooked medium shrimp
2 teaspoons sambal oelek
2 tablespoons chopped fresh coriander
2 tablespoons chopped lemongrass
6$^{1}/_{2}$oz (200g) wonton wrappers

SHRIMP STOCK

4 cups (32fl oz/1L) water
reserved shrimp shells
2 kaffir lime leaves or 1 teaspoon grated lime zest
2 pieces dried galangal
1in (2.5cm) piece fresh ginger, sliced

SOUP

1 tablespoon oil
2 teaspoons shrimp paste
1 small carrot, julienned
$^{1}/_{2}$ cup (2oz/60g) green peas
1 clove garlic, chopped
1 tablespoon lime juice
2 teaspoons fish sauce
1 tablespoon chopped fresh coriander

To make wontons, peel and devein the shrimp,
reserving shells for stock. Chop shrimp and combine
with sambal oelek, coriander and lemongrass in bowl.

Make about 4 wontons at a time. Lay wonton
wrappers on board and top with teaspoon of shrimp
mixture. Brush edge of rounds with water. Gather
edges together and pinch firmly to seal. Set aside.

To make shrimp stock, combine water, reserved
shrimp shells, lime leaves, galangal and ginger in large
saucepan and bring to boil. Simmer 15 minutes. Strain
into measuring cup and add water, if needed, to make
4 cups (32fl oz/1 litre).

To make soup, heat oil in large saucepan, add
shrimp paste, and cook over low heat 1 minute. Stir in
shrimp stock, carrot, peas, garlic, lime juice and fish
sauce. Bring to boil and simmer 5 minutes.

Add wontons and simmer 5 minutes, then stir in
coriander. Serve immediately.

SERVES 4

Wooden spoon from Corso del Fiori

Spoon a teaspoon of filling onto wonton wrapper.

Gather edges together and pinch firmly to seal.

RIGHT: Thai-Style Shrimp Wonton Soup

Yam and Coconut Cream Soup

This deliciously creamy soup is excellent for special occasions. If you prefer, use coconut milk instead of coconut cream to reduce the fat content.

1 tablespoon oil
1 small onion, finely chopped
$^1/_4$ teaspoon shrimp paste
$^1/_2$–1 small red chili, chopped
1 tablespoon chopped lemongrass
8oz (250g) yam, peeled and chopped
1$^1/_3$ cups (11fl oz/330ml) well-flavored
  chicken stock
1 cup (8fl oz/250ml) coconut cream
1 tablespoon fish sauce
6 large uncooked shrimp, peeled and deveined
a handful of small fresh basil leaves

Combine oil, onion, shrimp paste, chili and lemongrass in food processor and blend to paste consistency. Stir paste in large saucepan over low heat about 5 minutes.

Add yam, chicken stock, coconut cream and fish sauce, cover and simmer 20 minutes.

Add shrimp and basil and simmer until shrimp are just cooked, about 3 more minutes.

SERVES 4 AS AN ENTREE
OR
2 AS A MAIN COURSE

Beef Meatball and Cucumber Soup

The meatballs can be prepared a day ahead or frozen, uncooked, to save time.

MEATBALLS
5oz (150g) ground beef
1 small onion, finely chopped
1 tablespoon purchased or homemade green
  curry paste
1 tablespoon chopped lemongrass
SOUP
2 cups (16fl oz/500ml) well-flavored beef stock
1 clove garlic, chopped
1 tablespoon chopped lemongrass
$^3/_4$in (2cm) piece fresh ginger, finely shredded
1 tablespoon fish sauce
2 tablespoons lime juice
1 small green cucumber, peeled, seeded and
  thinly sliced
2oz (60g) fresh or dried fine egg noodles
4 green onions, sliced
1 red chili, chopped (optional)

To make meatballs, combine meatball ingredients in food processor and blend well. Shape into meatballs, using 2 teaspoons for each.

To make soup, combine stock, garlic, lemongrass, ginger, fish sauce and lime juice in large saucepan. Bring to boil, then simmer 5 minutes.

Add cucumber, noodles and meatballs and simmer until meatballs are cooked, about 5 minutes. Add green onions before serving and top with chopped red chili if you would like extra spice.

SERVES 4 AS AN ENTREE
OR
2 AS A MAIN COURSE

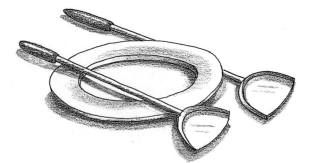

Mixed Vegetable Soup

You can use any selection of vegetables in this recipe.
I generally use a mixture of tiny broccoli florets,
shredded red cabbage, quartered mini corn, straw
mushrooms and green peas.

1 tablespoon oil
1/4 teaspoon shrimp paste
1 clove garlic, finely chopped
2 coriander roots, finely chopped
4 green onions, chopped
3 cups (24fl oz/750ml) well-flavored chicken or
*   vegetable stock*
1 cup (8fl oz/250ml) coconut milk
1 tablespoon fish sauce
8oz (250g) mixed chopped vegetables
2 tablespoons lime juice
2–4 teaspoons sambal oelek (to taste)
1 tablespoon chopped fresh coriander

Heat oil in saucepan. Add shrimp paste, garlic,
coriander roots and green onions and cook gently 1
minute.

Add stock, coconut milk and fish sauce and bring to
boil. Add vegetables and simmer about 10 minutes or
until vegetables are just tender. Stir in lime juice,
sambal oelek and coriander and serve immediately.

SERVES 4 AS AN ENTREE

OR

2 AS A MAIN COURSE

Hot and Sour Chicken Soup

A variation of tom yum khai, this soup is made simple
by using tom yum paste, readily available from
Asian food stores.

3 cups (24fl oz/750ml) well-flavored chicken stock
1–2 small green chilies, seeded and chopped
2 tablespoons finely chopped lemongrass
2 kaffir lime leaves or 1 teaspoon grated lime zest
1 tablespoon tom yum paste
1/2 cup (3 1/2oz/100g) drained canned straw
*   mushrooms*
1 chicken thigh fillet, thinly sliced
2 teaspoons fish sauce
1 tablespoon lime juice
1 tablespoon chopped fresh coriander
2 green onions, sliced

Combine chicken stock, chilies, lemongrass, lime
leaves, tom yum paste and mushrooms in pan. Bring to
boil, then boil, covered, 5 minutes.

Add chicken, fish sauce and lime juice and simmer
until chicken is cooked, about 3 minutes. Serve
sprinkled with coriander and green onions.

SERVERS 4 AS AN ENTREE

OR

2 AS A MAIN COURSE

Smoked Pork Soup with Rice and Yellow Mung Beans

This soup is a great meal in itself and will serve 2 people with hearty appetites.
Ask your butcher to cut the ham hock into 3 pieces and to trim as much fat as
possible from it. I have used jasmine rice in this recipe for its lovely aroma, but
long-grain white rice may be substituted. I found dried split yellow mung beans at
my local Asian food store, but if they're unavailable, substitute red lentils.

1lb (450g) ham hock
8 cups (64fl oz/2 L) water
1½in (3cm) piece fresh ginger, quartered
1 lime
2 green onions
2 teaspoons oil
2 tablespoons jasmine rice
1 clove garlic, crushed
1 tablespoon chopped fresh lemongrass
2 tablespoons dried split yellow mung beans
1 small onion, grated
2 teaspoons lime juice
1 green onion, chopped
1 tablespoon shredded fresh coriander

Combine ham, water and ginger in large saucepan and
bring to boil. Simmer, uncovered, 45 minutes,
skimming off any scum that may appear during
cooking. Strain stock, discarding ginger. Reserve ham
pieces and about 3½ cups (28fl oz/875ml) stock. Chop
ham and discard bones.

Using vegetable peeler, peel rind from lime. Cut
rind into thin strips. Cut green onions into thin strips
about 1½in (3cm) long.

Heat oil in wok or saucepan. Add rice, garlic and
lemongrass and stir-fry about 1 minute or until rice is
puffed and white and mixture is aromatic. Add
reserved stock, beans and onion, bring to boil and
simmer, partly covered, until the rice and beans are just
tender, about 10 minutes. Remove from heat and add
lime juice and ham. Serve sprinkled with lime rind
strips, green onion and coriander.

MAKES 2 LARGE SERVINGS

Reserve about 3½ cups stock; chop ham and discard
bones.

Cook until rice is puffed and white and mixture is
aromatic.

*RIGHT: Smoked Pork Soup with
Rice and Yellow Mung Beans*

Carved bamboo from Corso del Fiori

Noodles and Rice

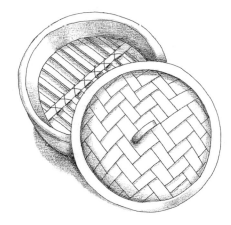

The variety of noodles used in Asian cooking allows for a wonderful selection of simple dishes to make with all types of delicious additions. Rice is the most important food in any traditional Asian meal. Small portions of superbly flavored dishes are served with the rice and used to add savor to it.

A typical meal will consist of three parts rice to two parts accompanying dishes. Always have plenty of steamed rice on hand to soak up the delicious sauces and juices.

Most of these rice and noodle dishes are quite filling and will serve up to four people as an accompaniment.

RIGHT: Egg Noodle and Vegetable Stir-Fry

Egg Noodle and Vegetable Stir-Fry

If you don't like the unique flavor of Chinese dried mushrooms, omit them and double the quantity of button mushrooms.

6 Chinese dried mushrooms
5oz (150g) ribbon or thick fresh egg noodles
1 tablespoon oil
1/4 teaspoon sesame oil
1 1/2oz (45g) fresh bean sprouts
1 small red bell pepper, thinly sliced
1 small yellow bell pepper, thinly sliced
2 1/2oz (75g) button mushrooms, thinly sliced
1/4 cup (2fl oz/60ml) sweet chili sauce
1 tablespoon light soy sauce

Place mushrooms in bowl, cover with hot water and let stand for 20 minutes. Drain well. Slice mushrooms, discarding tough stems.

Add noodles to large saucepan of boiling water and boil 3 minutes. Drain well, tossing in a little oil to keep noodles from sticking together.

Heat oils in wok or large frying pan. Add bean sprouts, peppers and mushrooms and stir-fry until peppers are almost soft. Add noodles and sauces and stir-fry until heated through and well combined.

SERVES 2 TO 4

Steamed Jasmine Rice

This is the staple of Thai eating. The rice should be tender and moist enough to stick together without being soggy. Use a large enough saucepan so that the rice and water mixture is only about 1in (2.5cm) deep before cooking; this will give the best results. Don't be tempted to lift the lid during the cooking or standing times – you will allow the heat and steam to escape.

1 cup (6 1/2oz/200g) jasmine rice
2 1/4 cups (18fl oz/560ml) water

Place rice in sieve and rinse under cold running water until water runs clear; drain well. Combine rice and water in heavy-based saucepan and stir over high heat until boiling; then reduce heat to simmer, cover tightly and allow to simmer 13 minutes without removing lid.

Remove from heat and let rice stand 10 minutes without removing lid, then uncover and fluff rice gently with fork before serving.

SERVES 2 TO 4

VARIATIONS

◆ Toss through 3 tablespoons chopped fresh coriander and 1/4 small chopped red pepper.
◆ Toss through 8 finely shredded fresh spinach leaves and 1/2 teaspoon sesame oil.

Thai Rice Balls

These rice balls can be deep-fried in hot oil if you prefer. I like the baking method, as it is easy to pop them into the oven and let them cook by themselves. Serve them with curries and stir-fries.

Steamed Jasmine Rice (page 44)
1 egg
1/2 cup (10oz/30g) chopped fresh coriander
1 tablespoon chopped lemongrass
1 teaspoon grated lime zest
2–4 teaspoons sambal oelek (to taste)
1 tablespoon fish sauce
2 tablespoons chopped fresh basil

Combine rice, egg, coriander, lemongrass, lime zest, sambal oelek, fish sauce and basil in bowl and mix well. Refrigerate mixture about 30 minutes or until cold. With lightly oiled hands, firmly roll mixture into balls using 2–3 tablespoons for each.

Arrange rice balls on oiled baking sheet and bake in 450°F (220°C) oven until crisp and lightly browned, about 20 minutes.

MAKES ABOUT 10

VARIATIONS
Add 2oz (60g) finely chopped cooked shrimp, finely chopped ham or flaked and well-drained canned crabmeat.

Quick Fried Noodles

Fresh rice noodles can be found in Asian food stores. They are usually found near the front counter or in the refrigerator packed in sealed plastic packages. If you are unable to buy them, substitute dried rice stick noodles, using the same cooking method.

8oz (250g) fresh rice noodles
2 tablespoons oil
2 cloves garlic, crushed
6 uncooked medium shrimp, peeled and deveined
2oz (60g) firm tofu, cubed
1 tablespoon oyster sauce
1 tablespoon fish sauce
2 tablespoons lemon juice
2 teaspoons sugar
2 tablespoons chopped roasted peanuts
1/2 teaspoon chili powder
4 green onions, chopped and fried until crisp fresh coriander leaves

Place noodles in heatproof bowl and cover with boiling water. Let stand 5 minutes, then drain well, tossing with a little oil to keep noodles from sticking together.

Meanwhile, heat oil in wok or large frying pan. Add garlic, shrimp and tofu and stir-fry until shrimp are just cooked. Add noodles, shrimp sauces, lemon juice, sugar, peanuts, chili powder and green onions, and stir-fry over high heat until heated through. Serve sprinkled with coriander leaves.

SERVES 2 TO 4

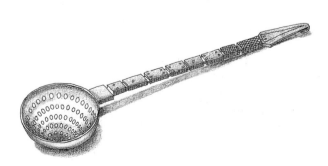

Rice and Shrimp Paste Omelet Rolls

These very flavorful rolls are something different to serve for breakfast or brunch.
Don't be put off by the strong smell of the shrimp paste. When it is cooked in a
dish it adds a lovely, typically Vietnamese flavor.

RICE FILLING
2 teaspoons oil
2 cloves garlic, crushed
2 teaspoons grated fresh ginger
1 small onion, finely chopped
½ teaspoon shrimp paste
1 tablespoon light soy sauce
1 cup (8fl oz/250ml) well-flavored chicken stock
½ cup (4oz/125g) uncooked long-grain rice

OMELETS
2 tablespoons oil
8 green onions, chopped
2 small red chilies, seeded and finely chopped
5 eggs, beaten
2 teaspoons fish sauce
½ cup (4fl oz/125ml) coconut cream

To make filling, heat oil in saucepan. Add garlic, ginger, onion and shrimp paste and stir-fry until aromatic. Add soy sauce and stock and bring to boil. Add rice, return to boil and boil 1 minute. Reduce heat to medium and simmer until nearly all liquid has evaporated and holes appear in surface of rice, about 3 minutes.

Cover pan tightly, reduce heat to lowest setting, and cook 20 minutes without removing lid. Remove from heat and let stand 10 minutes, then fluff with fork or chopsticks.

To make omelets, heat half of oil in a 9in (23cm) omelet pan. Add half of green onions and half of chilies and cook until onion turns bright green and mixture is aromatic.

Mix eggs, fish sauce and coconut cream. Pour half of mixture over green onions in pan, swirling pan so egg mixture completely covers bottom. Cook over low heat until omelet is just set.

Spoon half of rice filling into center of omelet and fold over sides to enclose. Slide onto plate and keep warm while preparing second omelet. Repeat procedure to make second omelet adding remaining oil to pan to avoid sticking.

SERVES 2

For filling, simmer rice until holes appear.

Cook egg mixture until omelet is just set.

RIGHT: Rice and Shrimp Paste Omelet Rolls

Seafood and Fresh Rice Noodle Toss

Substitute any seafood such as scallops, crab or oysters.

7oz (200g) white fish fillet
8 fresh asparagus spears
7oz (200g) uncooked shrimp, peeled and deveined
5 teaspoons fish sauce
1 tablespoon rice vinegar
3 cloves garlic, crushed
¼ teaspoon freshly ground black pepper
7oz (200g) fresh rice noodles
3 tablespoons oil
1 egg, lightly beaten
1 tablespoon chopped garlic chives
4 green onions, chopped
1 cup (2½oz/80g) bean sprouts
2 tablespoons roasted peanuts, chopped
1 small red chili, sliced
Fish Dipping Sauce (see page 155)

Cut fish fillet into 1¼in (3cm) pieces. Cut asparagus diagonally into 1½in (4cm) lengths.

Combine fish pieces, shrimp, 3 teaspoons fish sauce, vinegar, garlic and pepper in bowl. Refrigerate.

Add rice noodles to pan of boiling water and let stand 30 seconds. Drain and rinse under cold water.

Heat 1 tablespoon oil in wok or frying pan until very hot. Combine egg and remaining 2 teaspoons fish sauce and add to pan, swirling, to form a thin crepe. Cook until just set. Carefully lift onto paper towels to drain. Roll up, and cut into thin slices.

Heat 1 tablespoon oil in same wok, add seafood mixture and stir-fry until just cooked. Remove seafood and drain liquid from wok. Heat remaining oil in same wok. Add garlic chives, green onions and asparagus and stir-fry 2 minutes. Return seafood to wok with egg strips, noodles, bean sprouts and half of peanuts and stir-fry until well combined. Serve sprinkled with remaining peanuts and chili and drizzled with fish dipping sauce.

SERVES 2

Cellophane Noodles and Chili Vegetables

Any assortment of vegetables can be used in this recipe including red or green bell peppers, pumpkin or rutabaga, parsnip or turnip, instead of the ones I have suggested.

1½oz (50g) cellophane noodles
2 Chinese dried mushrooms
7oz (200g) daikon radish
1 small carrot
1 small cucumber
1 celery stalk, thinly sliced
4 green onions, sliced
¼ Chinese cabbage, finely shredded
1 tablespoon fresh mint leaves
2 tablespoons fresh coriander leaves
2 teaspoons toasted sesame seeds
1 teaspoon dried chili flakes
DRESSING
3 cloves garlic, crushed
rice vinegar
⅓ cup light soy sauce
2-3 teaspoons sesame oil
2 teaspoons fish sauce

Cover noodles with hot water in bowl and let stand 30 minutes. Drain well. Cover mushrooms with hot water in small bowl and let stand 30 minutes. Drain, discard stems and thinly slice mushrooms.

Halve radish lengthwise. Using vegetable peeler, cut radish and carrot into long thin ribbons. Run teeth of fork along length of cucumber, continuing all the way around, then thinly slice cucumber.

Combine noodles, mushrooms, radish, carrot, cucumber, celery, green onions, cabbage, mint, coriander, sesame seeds and chili flakes in a large bowl.

To make dressing, combine garlic, vinegar, soy sauce, sesame oil and fish sauce in jar and shake well.

Just before serving, drizzle dressing over the noodles and vegetables.

SERVES 2 TO 4

Glutinous Rice with Beans and Sesame Seeds

This dish traditionally has savory, semisweet flavor and is often eaten as a midmorning or afternoon snack, but I have made it to be served as an accompaniment. If you cannot find glutinous rice at your local Asian food store, cook plain steamed rice as directed in the following recipe.

¾ cup (6oz/185g) glutinous rice
3½ cups (20fl oz/875ml) water
2 tablespoons oil
2 cloves garlic, crushed
2 teaspoons fish sauce
1 cup (8fl oz/250ml) well-flavored chicken stock
¼ cup (2oz/60g) dried split yellow mung beans
2 teaspoons sesame seeds, toasted
1 tablespoon shredded coconut, toasted, or
*   2 tablespoons roasted unsalted peanuts*

Soak rice in plenty of cold water at least 8 hours or overnight. Drain, rinse and drain again.

Bring 1½ cups (12fl oz/375ml) water to boil in saucepan. Add rice and return to boil. Boil uncovered 1 minute, being careful that it doesn't boil over. Cover pan with lid and drain away as much liquid as possible. Return pan to low heat and cook, covered, 20 minutes. Remove from heat and let stand 10 minutes, then fluff with fork or chopsticks.

Meanwhile, prepare mung bean topping. Heat oil in wok or saucepan, add garlic and stir-fry 1 minute or until aromatic. Add fish sauce, stock, 2 cups (16 fl oz/500ml) water and mung beans and simmer, uncovered, until beans are tender and most of liquid has evaporated, about 20 minutes, adding more water if necessary.

Transfer rice to plate and top with mung bean mixture. Sprinkle with seeds and coconut or peanuts.

SERVES 2

Steamed Rice

This is the Vietnamese method of cooking rice. To double the quantity of rice, the proportions are 2½ cups (20fl oz/625ml) cold water to 2 cups (16oz/500g) rice.

1½ cups (12fl oz/375ml) cold water
1 cup (8oz/250g) long-grain rice or jasmine rice

Bring water to boil in medium-size heavy-based saucepan. Add rice and return to boil. Boil 1 minute, then reduce heat to medium and simmer until most of water has evaporated and holes appear in the surface of rice, about 3 minutes. Reduce heat to lowest setting (if you are using electric burners, have another burner already on lowest setting). Cover pan tightly and cook for 20 minutes. Remove from heat and let stand 10 minutes, then fluff with fork or chopsticks.

SERVES 2 TO 3

Southern Fried Rice

This colorful dish is simple to make. It is excellent to serve with barbecues or as part of a buffet dinner. You can make the rice several hours ahead and reheat it, covered, in the oven or microwave quite successfully.

2 tablespoons oil
1 small onion, thinly sliced
2 cloves garlic, crushed
1 tablespoon chopped lemongrass
¹/₂ teaspoon shrimp paste
1 small red bell pepper, thinly sliced
5oz (150g) green beans, chopped
2 cups (13oz/400g) cooked long-grain rice
1 tablespoon light soy sauce
2 teaspoons fish sauce
2–4 teaspoons sambal oelek (to taste)
3 tablespoons chopped fresh coriander

Heat oil in wok or large frying pan. Add onion, garlic, lemongrass, shrimp paste, pepper and beans and cook gently until onion is soft.

Add rice and stir-fry until heated through. Add remaining ingredients and stir-fry over high heat until well combined.

SERVES 2 TO 4

VARIATION
Any vegetables can be used in this dish, such as broccoli, asparagus or carrot sticks.

Fresh Rice Noodles in Thai Sauce

If fresh rice noodles are not available, you can use dried rice stick noodles instead. Follow the same method.

7oz (200g) fresh thick rice noodles
2 tablespoons oil
2 cloves garlic, crushed
1 tablespoon purchased or homemade red curry paste
1 tablespoon chopped lemongrass
6 green onions, chopped
5oz (150g) can coconut cream
1 tablespoon fish sauce

Place noodles in heatproof bowl and cover with boiling water. Let stand 10 minutes, then drain well, tossing with a little oil to keep noodles from sticking together.

Heat oil in wok. Add garlic, curry paste, lemongrass and green onions and cook gently until onion is soft. Add coconut cream, fish sauce and noodles and toss gently until heated through.

SERVES 2 TO 4

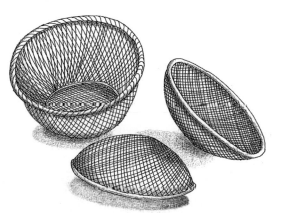

LEFT: Southern Fried Rice

Coconut shell spoon and stone dishes from Orson & Blake

Noodles with Basil, Coriander and Mint

This is a very simple dish to serve with curries, stir-fries or grilled fish or chicken. These noodles also make a tasty light meal when you don't feel like a heavy main course.

7oz (200g) fresh thin ribbon egg noodles
2 tablespoons oil
1 teaspoon grated fresh ginger
2 cloves garlic, finely chopped
2 teaspoons curry paste
1 tablespoon fish sauce
1 teaspoon oyster sauce
$1^1/_2$ cups $1^1/_2$oz (45g) mixed fresh basil, coriander and mint leaves
2 tablespoons coconut milk

Add noodles to large saucepan of boiling water and boil until tender, about 3 minutes. Drain well, tossing with a little oil to keep noodles from sticking together.

Heat oil in wok or large frying pan. Add ginger, garlic and curry paste and stir-fry gently until aromatic. Add noodles, sauces, herbs and coconut milk and stir-fry gently until heated through.

SERVES 2 TO 4

VARIATION

Toss in some chopped or thinly sliced Chinese barbecued pork and quartered mini corn.

Stir-Fried Rice with Barbecued Pork

Chinese barbecued pork can be found in Asian food stores and Chinese delis (where you will always find barbecued duck, pork and quail, among other delicious foods hanging in the window).

1 egg, beaten
1 tablespoon oil
2 teaspoons shrimp paste
6oz (180g) piece Chinese barbecued pork, thinly sliced
2 cloves garlic, crushed
2 teaspoons brown sugar
2 cups (13oz/400g) cooked long-grain rice
2 teaspoons fish sauce
6 green onions, sliced
2 tablespoons chopped fresh coriander
1 tablespoon sambal oelek
2 teaspoons light soy sauce

Oil wok and heat over high heat. Pour in egg and swirl around wok to coat thinly. Cook until omelet is set in center. Remove omelet from wok and cut into $^1/_2$in (1cm) strips.

Heat oil in wok, add shrimp paste and cook for a few seconds. Add pork, garlic and sugar and stir-fry until mixture is sizzling. Add rice, fish sauce, green onions, coriander, sambal oelek and soy sauce and stir-fry until heated through. Gently stir in omelet strips before serving.

SERVES 2 TO 4

RIGHT: From top: Noodles with Basil, Coriander and Mint; Stir-Fried Rice with Barbecued Pork

Rice Noodles with Chicken and Bell Pepper

Rice stick noodles are dried noodles that do not require cooking; all they need is a soak in hot water.

6oz (180g) rice stick noodles
2 tablespoons oil
2 single chicken breast fillets, sliced
1 small red bell pepper, thinly sliced
1 small green bell pepper, thinly sliced
2 cloves garlic, crushed
2 tablespoons chopped lemongrass
1 tablespoon grated fresh ginger
1 tablespoon oyster sauce
2 teaspoons fish sauce
1 tablespoon chopped roasted peanuts

Place noodles in heatproof bowl and cover with boiling water. Let stand 5 minutes, then drain well, tossing with a little oil to keep noodles from sticking together.

Heat oil in wok or large frying pan. Add chicken and stir-fry until lightly browned and just cooked, then remove from wok.

Add peppers, garlic, lemongrass and ginger to wok and stir-fry until peppers are tender. Add noodles, chicken and sauces and stir-fry over high heat until heated through. Sprinkle with peanuts and serve.

SERVES 2 TO 4

Bean Thread Vermicelli with Lime, Cucumber and Orange

You can also use regular vermicelli pasta in this recipe. It will give a different appearance to the final dish, however, as bean thread vermicelli become translucent when prepared.

3^1/$_2$oz (100g) bean thread vermicelli noodles
1 tablespoon oil
2 cloves garlic, crushed
1 tablespoon chopped lemongrass
^{1}/$_4$ teaspoon chili powder
1 small (7oz/200g) green cucumber,
    thinly sliced
2 teaspoons fish sauce
1 tablespoon sugar
2 tablespoons lime juice
1 orange, sectioned

Place vermicelli in heatproof bowl and cover with boiling water. Let stand 5 minutes, then cut into 1in (2.5cm) lengths with scissors. Drain well.

Heat oil in wok or large frying pan. Add garlic, lemongrass, chili powder and cucumber and stir-fry until cucumber is just softened. Add fish sauce, sugar and lime juice and toss well. Add noodles and orange sections and toss gently until heated through.

SERVES 2 TO 4

Chili and Coconut Rice

This dish is a richly flavored accompaniment for curries and stir-fries.

1 tablespoon oil
1 clove garlic, chopped
1 small onion, finely chopped
1/2 teaspoon shrimp paste
1 cup (7oz/200g) jasmine rice
1 1/2 cups (12fl oz/375ml) well-flavored
  chicken stock
3/4 cup (6fl oz/185ml) coconut milk
2 medium-size red chilies, seeded and chopped
2 tablespoons shredded fresh basil

Heat oil in heavy-based saucepan. Add garlic, onion and shrimp paste and cook gently, stirring often, for several minutes or until onion is very soft.

Meanwhile, place rice in sieve and rinse thoroughly under cold running water until water runs clear. Drain well.

Add rice, stock and coconut milk to onion mixture in saucepan and stir well. Bring to boil, stirring, then reduce heat, cover tightly and simmer 13 minutes without removing lid. Remove from heat and let stand 10 more minutes without removing lid.

Toss chilies and basil through with fork just before serving.

SERVES 2 TO 4

Brown Rice with Tofu and Ginger

1 cup (7oz/200g) brown rice
1 tablespoon oil
1/2 teaspoon sesame oil
1 tablespoon grated fresh ginger
2 cloves garlic, crushed
2 tablespoons chopped lemongrass
1 zucchini, grated
3 1/2oz (100g) firm tofu, cubed
1 tablespoon light soy sauce
1 tablespoon oyster sauce
3 tablespoons chopped fresh mint

Add rice to large saucepan of boiling water and boil uncovered 30 minutes. Drain well.

Heat oils in wok or large frying pan. Add ginger, garlic and lemongrass and cook gently 1 minute. Add zucchini and tofu and stir-fry gently until zucchini is soft. Add rice, sauces and mint and stir-fry until heated through.

SERVES 2 TO 4

VARIATIONS

◆ Add 2oz (60g) cooked cubed fish fillet and 2 tablespoons chopped fresh coriander before serving.

◆ Stir in 2oz (60g) roast beef strips and 1 chopped red chili before serving.

Lacquered bowls and woocen platter from Corso del Fiori

Steamed Rice with Pork, Shrimp and Vegetables

This is a very special way of preparing rice, usually reserved for special occasions. The various toppings can be arranged decoratively over a big platter of rice or served separately for each person to make his own choice. You will find barbecued pork at Chinese delis, or if you prefer, you can make your own by following the recipe for Oven-Baked Marinated Pork Fillet (see page 30).

1 cup (8fl oz/250ml) chicken stock or water
½ cup (4fl oz/125ml) coconut cream
1 cup (8oz/250g) uncooked long-grain rice
½ cup (2oz/60g) frozen green peas, thawed
1 Chinese dried mushroom
4 uncooked shrimp, peeled and deveined
5 teaspoons oil
2 green onions, sliced
1 tomato, finely chopped
2½ teaspoons fish sauce
1 egg, beaten
2½oz (75g) barbecued pork, thinly sliced
Pickled Carrot (see page 129)
Pickled Cucumber (see page 129)

Combine chicken stock and coconut cream in heavy-based medium saucepan and bring to boil. Add rice, bring to boil and boil uncovered 1 minute, stirring occasionally. Reduce heat to low (if you are using electric burners, transfer to another burner already on the lowest setting) and cook, covered, 20 minutes without removing lid.

Remove from heat and let stand 5 minutes, then fluff with fork or chopsticks. Stir peas into rice.

While rice is cooking, prepare shrimp sauce. Cover mushroom with hot water in small bowl and let stand 30 minutes. Drain, discard stem and slice mushroom thinly. Halve shrimp. Heat 3 teaspoons oil in medium saucepan, add green onions and stir-fry 1 minute. Add shrimp, tomato and 2 teaspoons fish sauce and simmer uncovered until sauce has thickened and the shrimp are cooked, about 2 minutes. Add mushroom.

Heat remaining 2 teaspoons oil in omelet pan or medium frying pan. Mix egg and remaining ½ teaspoon fish sauce and swirl pan so thin omelet is formed. Cook until just set. Slide omelet onto board, roll up and cut into ¼in (5mm) strips.

Spoon rice onto serving platter. Arrange shrimp sauce, barbecued pork, omelet strips and pickled vegetables over top, or serve each separately.

SERVES 2 TO 4

VARIATION
To make plain steamed rice, instead of using chicken stock and coconut cream, use 1 cup (8oz/250g) uncooked rice to 1½ cups (12fl oz/375ml) water. Follow same method as in recipe.

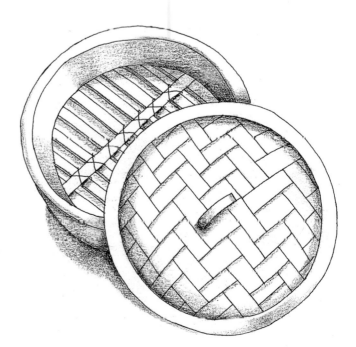

LEFT: Steamed Rice with Pork, Shrimp and Vegetables

Cutlery from Corso del Fiori

Wonton Noodle Strips with Eggplant and Bell Pepper

This colorful combination can be served hot as an accompaniment, or
a light lunch dish, or cold as a salad.

1 small eggplant

1 red bell pepper, quartered

*3¹/₂oz (100g) square or round wonton wrappers,
(about 3¹/₂in/9cm across), halved*

1 tablespoon oil

3 cloves garlic, thinly sliced

4 green onions, cut into short lengths

1–2 medium-size red chilies, shredded

1 tablespoon fish sauce

¹/₄ teaspoon sesame oil

1 tablespoon shredded fresh basil

Cut eggplant into thin slices, brush with oil and broil until browned and soft. Cut eggplant slices into wide strips.

Broil pepper skin side up until skin blackens and blisters. Place pepper in paper bag to cool.

Peel away and discard pepper skin and cut pepper into thick slices.

Drop wonton wrappers into large saucepan of boiling water and boil for 3 minutes. Drain, tossing with a little oil to keep wrappers from sticking together.

Heat 1 tablespoon oil in wok or large frying pan. Add garlic, green onions and chilies and cook gently until onions are soft. Add eggplant, pepper, wonton wrappers, fish sauce and sesame oil and stir-fry, tossing gently until heated through and well combined. Sprinkle with basil and serve. If serving cold, allow the dish to cool. Refrigerate up to one day and sprinkle with the basil before serving.

SERVES 2 TO 4

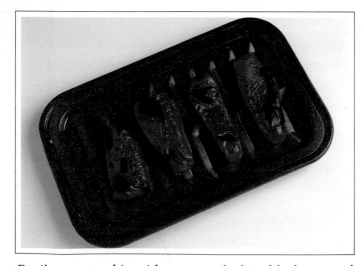

Broil pepper skin side up until skin blackens and blisters.

Peel away and discard skin and cut pepper into thick slices.

RIGHT: Wonton Noodle Strips with Eggplant and Bell Pepper

Beef, Tomato and Bamboo with Rice

1 tablespoon oil
11oz (350g) lean ground beef
3 cloves garlic, crushed
2 leeks, chopped
2 ripe tomatoes, finely chopped
1 parsnip, chopped
1 celery stalk, chopped
1/3 cup (2¹/2oz/80g) uncooked long-grain rice
1 tablespoon fish sauce
1 cup (8fl oz/250ml) well-flavored beef stock
1 can (7oz/227g) sliced bamboo shoots, drained
2 tablespoons chopped fresh mint

Heat oil in wok or saucepan. Add beef and stir-fry until well browned and dry. Add garlic, leeks, tomatoes, parsnip, celery and rice and stir-fry over high heat 2 minutes.

Add fish sauce and beef stock and bring to boil. Boil uncovered until most of liquid has evaporated and holes appear in surface of rice, about 3 minutes. Reduce heat to low (if using electric burners, transfer to another burner already on lowest setting), cover and cook 15 minutes without uncovering. Stir in bamboo shoots and mint before serving.

SERVES 2

Minted Rice with Chicken in Tomato Sauce

Equally good with ground chicken or pork. The sauce can be made a day ahead and reheated close to serving time.

1¹/2 cups (12fl oz/375ml) water
1 cup (8oz/250g) uncooked long-grain rice
1/4 cup (¹/2oz/15g) chopped fresh mint
1 tablespoon oil
8oz (250g) ground chicken
3 cloves garlic, crushed
1 onion, finely chopped
2 ripe tomatoes, finely chopped
3/4 cup (6fl oz/185ml) well-flavored chicken stock
2 teaspoons fish sauce
2 teaspoons tomato paste
1/4 teaspoon dried chili flakes

Bring water to boil in heavy-based medium saucepan. Add rice, return to boil and boil uncovered 1 minute. Reduce heat to medium and simmer uncovered until all of liquid has evaporated and holes appear in surface of rice, about 3 minutes. Cover tightly, reduce heat to low (if using electric burners, transfer to another burner already on lowest setting) and cook 20 more minutes. Remove from heat and let stand covered 10 minutes, then fluff with fork or chopsticks. Toss in mint and keep warm.

Heat oil in wok or saucepan. Add chicken and cook, stirring and breaking up any lumps, until dry and changed in color. Add garlic, onion and tomatoes and cook, stirring, until aromatic and tomatoes have softened.

Add chicken stock, fish sauce, tomato paste and chili flakes and bring to boil, then cover and simmer 7 minutes. Serve with minted rice.

SERVES 2

Lamb and Spinach with Soft Rice Noodles

Use any type of leafy greens such as bok choy, choy sum, chicory or Swiss chard.

10oz (300g) lamb fillet or beef skirt steak
5 teaspoons fish sauce
½ teaspoon freshly ground black pepper
7oz (200g) fresh rice noodles
10 fresh spinach leaves
3oz (100g) green beans
1 tablespoon sesame oil
4 cloves garlic, crushed
1 onion, cut into 8 wedges
4 shallots, halved
5 yellow teardrop tomatoes, halved
1 tablespoon light soy sauce
1 tablespoon oyster sauce
1 tablespoon chopped fresh garlic chives
¼ cup (2fl oz/60ml) water
2 tablespoons chopped fresh coriander

Cut lamb into thin strips. Combine meat with 2 teaspoons fish sauce and pepper in small bowl, cover and refrigerate while preparing remaining ingredients.

Cover noodles with boiling water in heatproof bowl. Let stand 30 seconds; drain. Cut spinach into thick shreds about 2in (5cm) wide. Cut beans into 1½in (4cm) lengths.

Heat sesame oil in wok or large frying pan. Add noodles and garlic and stir-fry until aromatic and noodles start to brown, about 2 minutes. Transfer to serving plate.

Reheat wok. Add lamb mixture and stir-fry 1 minute. Add onion and shallots and stir-fry 2 more minutes. Add beans and stir-fry 2 minutes, then add spinach, tomatoes, sauces (including remaining 3 teaspoons fish sauce), chives and water and stir-fry until spinach is just wilted. Return noodles to pan with coriander and toss well.

SERVES 2

Chicken and Rice Casserole

"Lovely legs" are chicken drumsticks without the skin and with the bottom part of the drumstick cut off.

3 Chinese dried mushrooms
4 cups (32fl oz/1L) water
2 chicken thigh fillets, skin removed
2 chicken drumsticks or "lovely legs," skin removed
1 tablespoon oil
3 cloves garlic, crushed
1 onion, finely chopped
½ cup (4oz/125g) long-grain rice
2 teaspoons light soy sauce
2 teaspoons fish sauce
¼ teaspoon freshly ground black pepper
3 green onions, chopped
1 tablespoon chopped fresh coriander
1 small red chili, seeded and finely chopped

Cover mushrooms with hot water in bowl and let stand 30 minutes. Drain, discard tough stems and thinly slice mushrooms.

Bring water to boil in medium saucepan. Add chicken pieces, bring to simmer and simmer, covered, 25 minutes. Remove chicken and reserve 1½ cups (12fl oz/ 375ml) stock.

Heat oil in wok or large saucepan. Add chicken, and cook until browned on all sides. Drain on paper towels. Add garlic and onion to wok and cook, stirring, about 1 minute or until aromatic. Add rice and stir-fry over high heat until just browned, about 2 minutes. Add reserved chicken stock, soy sauce, fish sauce, mushrooms and pepper and boil, uncovered, until most of liquid has evaporated, about 6 minutes.

Place chicken pieces on top of rice. Cover wok, reduce heat to low, cook 15 minutes without removing lid. Toss with green onions, coriander and chili before serving.

SERVES 2 TO 4

Pork and Coconut Curry with Noodles and Sprouts

1lb (450g) pork neck
3 spring (bulb) onions or large green onions
1 tablespoon oil
2 tablespoons chopped lemongrass
3 cloves garlic, crushed
1 tablespoon curry powder
1/4 teaspoon chili powder
1 3/4 cups (14fl oz/435ml) water
1 cup (8fl oz/250ml) well-flavored chicken stock
2 medium potatoes, peeled and quartered
3oz (100g) baby yellow squash, quartered
2 teaspoons cornstarch
2 teaspoons fish sauce
1/2 cup (4fl oz/125ml) coconut cream
4oz (125g) bundle fresh thin egg noodles, cut
   into thirds
chopped fresh coriander
fresh chili strips
1/4 cup (1oz/30g) mung bean sprouts

Trim any excess fat from pork and cut pork into 1 1/2in (4cm) pieces. Cut tender green tops of onions into 3/4in (2cm) sections; halve onion bulbs.

Heat oil in wok or frying pan. Cook pork in batches until browned; drain on paper towels. Drain all but about 2 teaspoons oil from wok.

Add lemongrass, garlic, curry powder and chili powder to wok and cook, stirring, 1 minute or until aromatic. Return pork to wok with water and chicken stock and bring to boil. Reduce heat and simmer, covered, 20 minutes. Add onions, potatoes and squash and simmer, covered, 20 minutes.

Blend cornstarch with fish sauce and coconut cream and stir into wok. Add noodles and simmer, covered, 5 minutes. Sprinkle with chopped coriander and chili strips and serve mung bean sprouts on the side.

SERVES 2 TO 4

Crisp Noodles and Alfalfa

I have generally avoided deep-fried foods in this book, but for this recipe I couldn't resist deep-frying the rice vermicelli to obtain that wonderful crisp texture that makes the dish so delicious. You may use any leftover cooked meats instead of the chicken and shrimp, and if you can't find black sesame seeds at your local Asian food store, toast some white sesame seeds and use those instead.

oil for deep-frying
3oz (100g) rice vermicelli
1/4 cup (1/2oz/15g) alfalfa sprouts
3oz (100g) cooked chicken, chopped
8 large cooked shrimp, peeled and chopped
8 cherry tomatoes, halved
1 tablespoon chopped fresh coriander
1 tablespoon chopped fresh mint
1 tablespoon black sesame seeds
DRESSING
1/4 cup (2fl oz/60ml) oil
1 small red chili, seeded and finely chopped
1 tablespoon grated fresh ginger
1 1/2 tablespoon fish sauce
1/4 cup (2fl oz/60ml) lime juice
2 teaspoons sesame oil
2 teaspoons honey

Heat oil in deep-fryer or large saucepan until hot. Add rice vermicelli in 2 batches; it will quickly turn white and puff up. Remove from pan with slotted spoon and drain on paper towels. Place on serving plate.

To make dressing, combine all dressing ingredients in screw-top jar and shake well.

Serve rice vermicelli with alfalfa, chicken, shrimp, tomatoes, coriander, mint and sesame seeds. Drizzle with dressing just before serving.

SERVES 2 TO 4

RIGHT: From top: Pork and Coconut Curry with Noodles and Sprouts; Crisp Noodles and Alfalfa

Main Courses

This section has been planned with all styles of eating in mind. There is a great variety of dishes, from the traditional to the elegant, and some are very appropriate for family fare. In a traditional Asian meal, the meat, fish or poultry is not the main feature but is served to accompany and flavor the rice. Serve one main course for every two people at an Asian meal, with a large quantity of steamed rice, a soup, a vegetable dish and a noodle or rice dish. All the dishes should be placed in the center with everyone helping himself. The main courses in this section serve two on their own; some will serve four as part of an Asian meal.

RIGHT: Chili Garlic Quail with Ginger

Chili Garlic Quail with Ginger

Although a little fussy to eat, quail are absolutely delicious smothered with a hot chili marinade and baked, grilled or barbecued to perfection. Use less sambal oelek for a milder flavor.

4–6 quail
3 cloves garlic, crushed
1 small onion, grated
3 tablespoons sambal oelek
1 tablespoon light soy sauce
2 teaspoons grated fresh ginger
2 teaspoons brown sugar
1 tablespoon oil

Using sharp kitchen scissors, cut quail in half, cutting away and discarding backbones and necks (if attached). (Scissors are easier to use than a sharp knife as they give you a little more control over cutting through the bones.)

Combine all remaining ingredients in bowl and mix well. Using pastry brush, brush mixture generously over pieces of quail. Place quail in non-aluminum dish and pour any remaining marinade over. Cover and refrigerate at least 4 hours, preferably overnight.

Place quail in single layer, skin side up, on wire rack over roasting pan. Bake in 375°F (190°C) oven, brushing with any marinade remaining in dish, until the quail are cooked through, about 30 minutes.

SERVES 2 TO 4

VARIATION
Chicken legs or thighs can be substituted for quail. They will need about 40 minutes to cook through.

Thai Green Curry Chicken

There are many variations of green curry chicken. This version uses a good-quality purchased curry paste. Buy it from the supermarket or an Asian food store.

12oz (375g) chicken thigh fillets
2 tablespoons oil
2 cloves garlic, crushed
1 teaspoon shrimp paste
1 tablespoon purchased or homemade green
    curry paste
1 tablespoon chopped lemongrass
2 kaffir lime leaves or 1 teaspoon grated lime zest
1 tablespoon fish sauce
$^{1}/_{2}$ cup (4fl oz/125ml) water
$^{1}/_{2}$ cup (4fl oz/125ml) coconut cream
$^{1}/_{2}$ cup (2oz/60g) peas
7oz (200g) broccoli, cut into florets
2 tablespoons fresh coriander leaves
1 tablespoon shredded fresh basil
Steamed Jasmine Rice (page 44)

Cut any excess fat from chicken fillets, then cut fillets in half. Heat oil in wok or large frying pan. Add chicken in batches and cook until browned all over. Remove from wok and drain on paper towels.

Add garlic, shrimp paste and curry paste to wok and cook gently for a few seconds. Stir in lemongrass, lime leaves, fish sauce, water and coconut cream and bring to boil. Add chicken pieces and simmer 10 minutes, partially covered.

Add peas and broccoli and simmer 5 minutes. Stir in coriander and basil and serve immediately with jasmine rice.

SERVES 2 TO 4

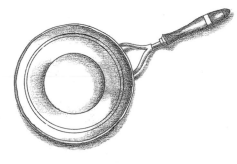

Braised Chicken Drumsticks

I always prefer to remove the skin and fat from chicken if it is in a braise such as this. The chicken is delicious to eat to the last mouthful. Serve this with rice or noodles.

2 cloves garlic, chopped
1 small onion, chopped
1–2 red chilies, seeded and chopped
$^1/_4$ teaspoon ground cumin
$^1/_4$ teaspoon ground coriander
$^1/_4$ teaspoon ground turmeric
$^1/_4$ teaspoon five spice powder
1 teaspoon shrimp paste
6 chicken drumsticks
2 tablespoons oil
$^1/_2$ cup (4fl oz/125ml) well-flavored chicken stock
$^1/_2$ cup (4fl oz/125ml) coconut milk
1 tablespoon chopped fresh coriander

Combine garlic, onion, chilies, cumin, coriander, turmeric, five spice powder and shrimp paste in food processor and grind to paste consistency. Remove skin and any fat from chicken. Heat oil in wok or large frying pan. Add chicken and cook until browned all over, then remove from wok.

Add spice paste to wok and cook gently 1 minute. Add chicken, stock and coconut milk, cover and simmer until the chicken is cooked through, about 30 minutes, stirring and turning chicken occasionally. Sprinkle with coriander.

SERVES 2 TO 4

Stir-Fried Chicken and Asparagus

If you cannot find good fresh asparagus, substitute green beans or snow peas.

4 chicken thigh fillets
1 tablespoon oil
12 spears fresh asparagus, cut into short lengths
2 cloves garlic, crushed
$^1/_4$ teaspoon shrimp paste
$^1/_2$ teaspoon grated fresh ginger
2 medium-size fresh red chilies, finely chopped
1 teaspoon light soy sauce
1 tablespoon fish sauce
2 tablespoons well-flavored chicken stock
$^1/_2$ cup ($^1/_2$oz/15g) shredded fresh basil

Remove any fat from chicken. Cut chicken into thin slices. Heat oil in wok or large frying pan. Add chicken and asparagus and stir-fry until chicken is almost cooked. Add garlic, shrimp paste, ginger and chilies and stir-fry a few seconds.

Stir in soy sauce, fish sauce and stock and stir until boiling and well combined. Gently toss in basil, then serve immediately.

SERVES 2 TO 4

Spicy Roasted Duck Breast Rolls

This dish can look very impressive at a dinner party and is easy to prepare.
The spices go well with duck, but if duck is unavailable, substitute
chicken breast fillets.

2 single duck breasts
1 tablespoon roasted peanuts, finely ground
2 green onions, finely chopped
3 teaspoons grated fresh ginger
2 teaspoons chopped fresh coriander
2 cloves garlic, crushed
½ teaspoon five spice powder
½ teaspoon cinnamon
1 tablespoon honey
1 teaspoon tomato paste
½ teaspoon freshly ground black pepper
1 tablespoon light soy sauce
1 teaspoon sesame oil
2 cloves garlic, sliced
10 leaves choy sum, halved
2½oz (75g) oyster mushrooms
¼ cup (2fl oz/60ml) water

Cut away and discard the duck wing by cutting through joint. Carefully run sharp knife along breastbone of duck, continuing with short cuts until the meat comes away from bone. Remove skin from breast fillet. Repeat with other duck breast. With flat side of knife or with meat mallet, flatten out each breast until about ½in (1cm) thick.

Combine peanuts, green onions, 1 teaspoon ginger and coriander in bowl. Divide peanut mixture between duck breasts and spread evenly over surface. Roll up duck breasts tightly from short end to form a roll; secure with toothpicks. Blend crushed garlic, 2 teaspoons ginger, spices, honey, tomato paste, pepper and soy sauce and brush over rolls, reserving about 1½ tablespoons for vegetables. Place duck rolls on baking sheet and bake in 350°F (180°C) oven 35 minutes, brushing during cooking with any remaining spice mixture.

Meanwhile, heat sesame oil in wok or frying pan. Add sliced garlic and reserved spice mixtures and stir about 1 minute or until aromatic. Add choy sum, mushrooms and water and stir-fry until choy sum is just wilted. Slice rolls and serve with vegetables.

SERVES 2

Terracotta platter with shell inlay from Corso del Fiori

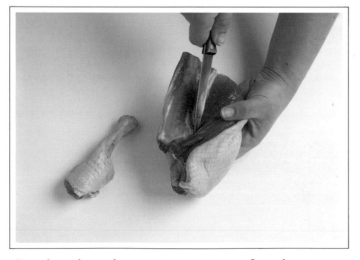

Cut along breastbone to remove meat from bones.

Roll up duck breast tightly from short end.

RIGHT: Spicy Roasted Duck Breast Rolls

Lemongrass and Chili Chicken

The lemongrass and chili give this dish a very fresh and spicy flavor. It is especially good eaten with some Pickled Carrot, Daikon Radish or Cucumber (see page 129). I have used shallot oil which I store in my pantry, for extra flavor, but you can use vegetable oil instead.

1 tablespoon lime juice
1 tablespoon chopped lemongrass
1 tablespoon grated fresh ginger
1 teaspoon red chili flakes
1 onion, grated
2 cloves garlic, crushed
1 tablespoon sugar
1 tablespoon fish sauce
2 chicken thigh cutlets
2 chicken drumsticks
2 tablespoons Shallot Oil (see page 155)

Using blender or mortar and pestle, blend lime juice, lemongrass, ginger, chili flakes, onion, garlic, sugar and fish sauce to smooth paste.

Remove the skin from chicken. Make 2 cuts in each piece of chicken at thickest part. Brush paste all over chicken pieces and into cuts. Cover and refrigerate at least 3 hours or overnight to allow flavors to develop. Cut 2 pieces of foil into 6½in (16cm) squares. Place cutlet and drumstick in center of each piece of foil and fold up ends to form package. Arrange on baking sheet and bake in 375°F (190°C) oven 30 minutes. Open package, then bake 30 more minutes or until chicken is tender, brushing with shallot oil to keep chicken from drying out.

SERVES 2

Baked Chicken Strips with Ginger and Tomato

This is a very light and healthy dish best served with lots of steamed rice to soak up the delicious juices.

2 Chinese dried mushrooms
7oz (200g) chicken thigh fillets
1½in (3cm) piece fresh ginger
4 leaves choy sum or fresh spinach,
  finely shredded
3 green onions, chopped
2 medium-size ripe tomatoes, chopped
1 tablespoons tomato paste
1 tablespoon fish sauce

Soak mushrooms in hot water 30 minutes. Discard stems and slice caps thinly.

Cut chicken into strips ¼in (5mm) thick. Cut ginger into long thin julienne. Boil or steam choy sum until just wilted. Refresh under cold water; drain.

Combine mushrooms, chicken, ginger, green onion, tomatoes, paste and sauce in 5 cup (40fl oz/1.25L) baking dish and bake in a 350°F (180°C) oven until the chicken is cooked, about 45 minutes. Stir in choy sum.

SERVES 2 TO 4

VARIATIONS
♦ In place of chicken, use lean pork or lamb cut into strips.
♦ Fish fillets such as snapper or perch, cut into large pieces, can be substituted for chicken. Reduce cooking time to 30 minutes or until fish is cooked, adding 1 tablespoon lime juice at end of cooking time.

Barbecued Chicken Livers and Potatoes

Something perfect for a barbecue, you can serve the livers as appetizers or as a main meal with potatoes as I have suggested, and perhaps with Grapefruit, Sprout and Cucumber Salad (see page 132). The livers can be prepared ahead of time.

1 tablespoon grated fresh ginger
4 cloves garlic, crushed
2 tablespoons sweet chili sauce
12oz (350g) chicken livers, trimmed
2 medium potatoes
2 tablespoons fresh coriander leaves
Fish Dipping Sauce (see page 155)

Combine ginger, garlic and chili sauce in bowl, add chicken livers and stir until well coated. Cover and refrigerate 1 hour.

If using new potatoes, scrub them well and do not peel. Cut into slices ¼in (5mm) thick.

Barbecue or grill livers and potatoes over medium heat until browned and cooked through. Sprinkle livers with coriander leaves and serve with fish dipping sauce.

SERVES 2

VARIATION
Quartered chicken breast fillets or lamb scallops can be substituted for livers if you prefer.

Roasted Honey-Spiced Quail

These quail are best eaten with your fingers. You may find that just one quail each is not enough, so double the recipe if you have a big appetite. They are just as delicious eaten cold and served with Vegetable Platter with Dipping Sauce (see page 142).

2 quail
3 green onions, finely chopped
1 tablespoon grated fresh ginger
3 cloves garlic, crushed
pinch chili powder
2 tablespoons honey
2 tablespoons light soy sauce
1 tablespoon rice vinegar
crushed coriander seeds (optional)

Using sharp kitchen scissors, cut quail along either side of backbone and open out flat. Tuck wings behind breast bones.

With mortar and pestle, grind the green onion, ginger, garlic and chili powder together to form paste. Combine paste with honey, soy sauce and vinegar in shallow dish and mix well. Add quail, spooning marinade over. Cover and refrigerate overnight to allow flavors to develop.

Place quail breast side up on wire rack in roasting pan. Add some water to keep the juices from burning during cooking. Bake quail in 375°F (190°C) oven until cooked through, about 30 minutes, basting frequently with any remaining marinade. Sprinkle with crushed coriander before serving.

SERVES 2

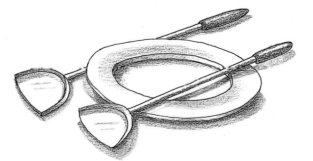

~ Tip ~
A simple way to crush the coriander seeds is by grinding them in short bursts in an electric coffee grinder. A blender or mortar and pestle also works well.

Marinated Chicken with Julienne Vegetables

2 single chicken breast fillets
2 tablespoons oil
2 cloves garlic, crushed
1 tablespoon light soy sauce
1/2 teaspoon sugar
2 teaspoons purchased or homemade
* red curry paste*
1/4 cup (2fl oz/60ml) lime juice
1 carrot
1/2 small zucchini
1/2 long baby eggplant
1/2 small yellow bell pepper
1/2 small red bell pepper
1 1/2 oz (50g) snow peas
1 tablespoon chopped fresh coriander

Place chicken in nonaluminum dish. Combine oil, garlic, soy sauce, sugar, curry paste and lime juice and pour half of mixture over chicken. Turn chicken to coat with marinade. Cover and refrigerate 2 hours.

Cut carrot, zucchini, eggplant and peppers into fine julienne. Cut snow peas in half diagonally.

Grill or barbecue chicken until browned and cooked through. While chicken is cooking, heat remaining marinade in wok or large frying pan, add prepared vegetables and stir until vegetables are almost cooked. Toss with coriander. Slice chicken and serve on bed of vegetables.

SERVES 2 TO 4

Chicken with Chinese Greens and Coconut Cream

This dish has the beautiful creamy coconut flavor so typical of Thai cuisine. Use bok choy or choy sum Chinese greens, available from Asian food stores and produce markets. Serve this with Steamed Jasmine Rice (page 44).

2 single chicken breast fillets
1 small bunch Chinese greens
2 tablespoons oil
1/2 teaspoon shrimp paste
2 fresh coriander roots, finely chopped
1 tablespoon chopped lemongrass
1 clove garlic, finely chopped
2 small fresh red chilies, thinly sliced
1 tablespoon fish sauce
1 teaspoon sambal oelek
3/4 cup (6fl oz/185ml) coconut cream
2 tablespoons shredded fresh basil
1 tablespoon fresh coriander leaves

Cut chicken into 1/2in (1cm) strips. Wash Chinese greens well, then remove stems and cut into 2in (5cm) lengths. Shred leaves coarsely.

Heat the oil in wok or frying pan and cook chicken in batches, turning, turning once, just until lightly browned. Place chicken in bowl and set aside.

Reheat wok. Add shrimp paste, coriander roots, lemongrass and garlic and cook gently, stirring, until quite aromatic. Stir in chilies, fish sauce, sambal oelek and coconut cream with chicken and Chinese greens stems. Cover and simmer until chicken is cooked through, about 8 minutes. Add Chinese greens leaves and basil and toss gently until leaves are just wilted. Sprinkle with coriander and serve.

SERVES 2 TO 4

*RIGHT: Chicken with Chinese
Greens and Coconut Cream*

Chicken Noodle Lettuce Cups

2 single chicken breast fillets
2 teaspoons dark soy sauce
1 teaspoon fish sauce
2½oz (75g) rice vermicelli
2 tablespoons oil
8 choy sum leaves or fresh spinach leaves
4 Boston lettuce leaves
1 small carrot, julienned
1 tablespoon shredded fresh coriander leaves
1 tablespoon shredded fresh mint leaves
1 tablespoon roasted peanuts, chopped
Dressing
1 small red chili, seeded and finely chopped
2 cloves garlic, crushed
1 tablespoon honey
1 tablespoon rice vinegar
2 tablespoons lime juice
2 tablespoons fish sauce
2 tablespoons water

Combine chicken, soy sauce and fish sauce in bowl, cover and refrigerate overnight.

Cover rice vermicelli with boiling water in bowl and let stand 30 minutes. Drain well, then cut into short lengths.

Heat some of the oil in wok or frying pan. Add choy sum and stir-fry until just wilted. Stir in rice vermicelli. Spoon some of mixture into each lettuce leaf. Sprinkle with carrot.

For dressing, combine all dressing ingredients in jar and shake well.

Heat remaining oil in wok. Add chicken and cook until well browned on both sides and cooked through, about 8 minutes. Slice chicken thinly and arrange over rice vermicelli mixture in lettuce cups. Sprinkle with coriander, mint and peanuts and drizzle with dressing.

SERVES 2

Chicken Curry with Carrot and Parsnip

2 tablespoons chopped lemongrass
4 cloves garlic, crushed
1 small onion, grated
1 small red chili, chopped
1 tablespoon purchased or homemade red
  curry paste
1 tablespoon curry powder
2 teaspoons shrimp paste
1 single chicken breast, on the bone, skin removed
2 chicken thighs, skin removed
2 tablespoons oil
1 large onion, cut into 8 wedges
1 large ripe tomato, chopped
1½ cups (12fl oz/375ml) well-flavored chicken stock
½ cup (4fl oz/125ml) water
1 tablespoon fish sauce
1 carrot, chopped
1 parsnip, chopped
⅔ cup (5½fl oz/165ml) coconut milk
1 tablespoon roasted peanuts, chopped
1 fresh green chili, chopped

Combine lemongrass, garlic, grated onion, red chili, red curry paste, curry powder and shrimp paste in food processor and blend until smooth. Using sharp knife or cleaver, cut chicken breast in half. Make 2 cuts into thighs at thickest part. Brush half of curry paste all over chicken pieces and into cuts. Cover, let stand 1 hour.

Heat some oil in wok or frying pan and brown chicken in batches, adding extra oil as needed. Drain on paper towels. Drain excess oil from wok, add remaining curry paste and cook until aromatic. Add onion and tomato and stir-fry until tomato is soft, about 3 minutes.

Add chicken thighs, stock and water and simmer, uncovered, 30 minutes. Add fish sauce, breast pieces, carrot and parsnip and simmer, uncovered, 30 minutes or until chicken is cooked. Stir in coconut milk and bring to boil. Serve sprinkled with peanuts and chili.

SERVES 2

LEFT: From left: Chicken Noodle Lettuce Cups;
Chicken Curry with Carrot and Parsnip

Barbecued Peppered Chicken with Chili Sauce

This is a simple dish to make. The chicken can be marinated 2 days ahead.

2 single chicken breast fillets
2 cloves garlic, crushed
2 teaspoons grated fresh ginger
1/2 teaspoon cracked black peppercorns
2 tablespoons chopped fresh coriander
1 tablespoon chopped lemongrass
1 tablespoon light soy sauce
1 tablespoon oil
CHILI SAUCE
1 small red chili, finely chopped
1/3 cup (2 1/2fl oz/80ml) white vinegar
pinch salt
1 tablespoon sugar
1 clove garlic, crushed

Trim any fat from chicken. Place chicken in non-aluminum dish. Combine garlic, ginger, peppercorns, coriander and lemongrass in bowl; stir in soy sauce and oil.

Pour marinade over chicken and turn chicken to coat well. Cover and refrigerate at least 3 hours, preferably overnight to allow flavors to develop.

For chili sauce, combine all ingredients in small saucepan and simmer uncovered 3 minutes. Cool. Barbecue or broil chicken until browned and just cooked through. Serve with chili sauce.

SERVES 2

Chicken Livers with Chili

Cook this dish at the last minute. The chicken livers make a delicious combination with authentic Thai flavors. Use bok choy or choy sum Chinese greens, available from Asian food stores and produce markets.

14oz (400g) chicken livers
4 lemon wedges
1 tablespoon oil
1 onion, thinly sliced
2 cloves garlic, crushed
1 medium-size red chili, thinly sliced
1 medium-size green chili, thinly sliced
2 tablespoons coconut milk
6 large Chinese greens leaves, shredded
1 tablespoon fish sauce
2 tablespoons chopped fresh coriander

Soak chicken livers in water to cover with lemon wedges for 30 minutes. Drain well and peel away any fine white membrane from livers. Cut away any fat, then halve livers.

Heat oil in frying pan. Add onion and garlic and cook gently several minutes until onion is very soft. Add livers and cook, turning occasionally, until almost cooked through.

Add chilies, coconut milk, Chinese greens and fish sauce and stir gently until greens are wilted and livers are just cooked through (don't overcook or they will become dry). Serve sprinkled with coriander.

SERVES 2 TO 4

LEFT: From top: Barbecued Peppered Chicken with Chili Sauce; Chicken Livers with Chili

Stuffed Cornish Hens with Nutty Cinnamon Rice

This very special Laotian dish would be stunning for a dinner party and is a must for an Indochinese banquet. This quantity will serve up to four people; the stuffing is quite filling. Include soup and salad to complete the meal.

2 teaspoons oil
2 cloves garlic, crushed
1 onion, finely chopped
1 teaspoon fennel seeds
½ teaspoon dried chili flakes
½ teaspoon cinnamon
8oz (250g) ground pork
2 tablespoons roasted peanuts, finely chopped
2 tablespoons uncooked long-grain rice
¾ cup (6fl oz/185ml) coconut cream
1 tablespoon chopped fresh mint
2 Cornish hens, about 1¼lb (600g) each
1⅔ cups (13fl oz/410ml) additional coconut cream
2 cups (16fl oz/500ml) water
2 teaspoons fish sauce
1 teaspoon curry powder
2 red chilies, sliced
chopped peanuts (optional)

Heat oil in wok or frying pan. Add garlic, onion, fennel seeds, chili and cinnamon and stir-fry until aromatic. Add pork and stir-fry until it changes color. Stir in peanuts and rice. Add coconut cream and bring to boil, then cover, reduce heat to low and cook for 10 minutes. Uncover, stir in mint and cool.

Spoon stuffing mixture into cavities of hens, forcing any remaining stuffing under skin around necks. Sew cavities closed or secure with toothpicks. Secure legs with kitchen string and tuck wings behind backs.

Combine additional coconut cream, water, fish sauce and curry powder in saucepan just large enough to fit both hens. Bring to boil. Add hens and simmer, covered, until the hens are cooked through, about 45 minutes, turning birds once during cooking.

Remove hens from pan and keep warm. Return pan to heat and simmer pan juices, uncovered, over medium heat about 15 minutes or until thickened slightly and reduced to about 1½ cups (12fl oz/375ml) sauce. Using sharp kitchen scissors and knife, cut down centers of birds. Serve with sauce, sprinkled with sliced chilies and extra chopped peanuts if desired.

SERVES 2 TO 4

VARIATION

If Cornish hens are unavailable, substitute a small chicken.

RIGHT: Stuffed Cornish hens with Nutty Cinnamon Rice

Chicken with Thai Seasoning

2 single chicken breast fillets

8 large fresh spinach leaves

2 teaspoons grated lime zest

1 tablespoon chopped fresh coriander

1 teaspoon sambal oelek

oil

SAUCE

2 tablespoons white vinegar

1 teaspoon brown sugar

$^1/_2$ teaspoon cornstarch

1 tablespoon water

$^1/_4$ teaspoon grated lime zest

2 teaspoons small fresh coriander leaves

$^1/_2$ small red chili, seeded and thinly sliced

Steamed Jasmine Rice (see page 44)

Remove tenderloin fillet from underside of each chicken fillet. Chop tenderloin fillets very finely, place in bowl and set aside.

Cut pocket into side of each chicken fillet without cutting all the way through.

Drop spinach into saucepan of boiling water, until just wilted. Drain and rinse under cold water, then drain on paper towels. Chop spinach and add to chopped chicken in bowl. Add lime zest, coriander and sambal oelek and mix well.

Push spinach seasoning into pockets in chicken fillets, then toothpick or skewer openings firmly together to seal.

Brush fillets with oil and place on baking sheet. Bake in 350°F (180°C) oven about 20 minutes or until chicken is cooked through.

While chicken is cooking, prepare sauce. Combine vinegar and sugar in small saucepan. Combine cornstarch and water and add to vinegar mixture. Stir over heat until mixture boils and thickens. Add remaining ingredients and mix well. Slice chicken and serve with sauce and jasmine rice.

SERVES 2

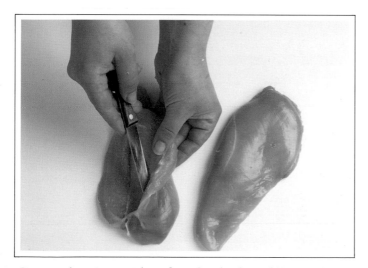

Cut pocket into side of each chicken fillet without cutting all the way through.

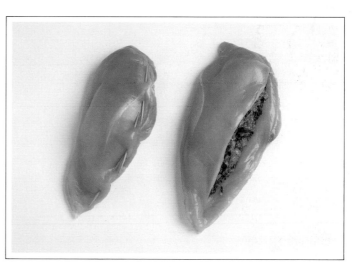

Toothpick or skewer openings together.

RIGHT: Chicken with Thai Seasoning

Woven basket from Orson & Blake

Tofu and Pork Stack with Bean Sauce

This dish looks very impressive for a dinner party and is a different way of using tofu. The stacks can be cut into halves or even quarters to serve more people.

1 tablespoon dried shrimp
1/2 block (7oz/225g) firm or hard tofu
2 cloves garlic, crushed
8oz (250g) ground pork
3 green onions, finely chopped
2 teaspoons fish sauce
1 tablespoon oyster sauce
1/2 teaspoon oil or Chili Oil (see page 154)
coriander sprigs
BEAN SAUCE
2/3 cup (5 1/2 fl oz/165ml) water
2 teaspoons fish sauce
1 teaspoon bean sauce
1 tablespoon tomato paste
1 teaspoon sugar
1 teaspoon cornstarch

Cover dried shrimp with hot water in small bowl. Let stand 30 minutes, then drain and chop finely. Drain tofu well and pat dry with paper towels. Cut into slices ½in (1.5cm) thick. You will need 4 slices measuring about 4in x 2½in (10cm x 6cm).

Combine garlic, pork, green onions, fish sauce and shrimp in bowl. Spread half of pork mixture over one of tofu slices and top with another tofu slice to form sandwich. Repeat with remaining pork mixture and tofu.

Place stacks on lightly greased baking sheet. Combine oyster sauce and oil and brush over stack. Bake in a 375°F (190°C) oven until the pork mixture is cooked, about 30 minutes, brushing with any remaining oyster sauce mixture.

For bean sauce, combine water, fish sauch, bean sauce, tomato paste, sugar and cornstarch in small saucepan and bring to boil. Simmer uncovered 1 minute. Serve stacks with bean sauce and garnish with coriander.

SERVES 2

VARIATION
Substitute ground chicken for pork. Add some finely chopped chili to the meat mixture if you would like dish hot and spicy

Glazed Pork Ribs with Bell Peppers

1lb (450g) pork spareribs
2 teaspoons oil
1 teaspoon shrimp paste
2 tablespoons sugar
1 1/2 tablespoons water
1 onion, cut into 8 wedges
3 cloves garlic, sliced
1 small red bell pepper, chopped
1 small green bell pepper, chopped
2 1/2 oz (75g) sugar snap peas
1 1/2 tablespoons light soy sauce
1 tablespoon chopped fresh coriander

Cut ribs into 2 rib sections. Heat oil in large frying pan and cook ribs about 30 minutes, turning, until browned and cooked through. Drain on paper towels.

Drain all but 1 tablespoon fat from pan. Add shrimp paste, sugar and water and stir until sugar has dissolved. Add onion, garlic, peppers and sugar snap peas and cook, stirring, until the vegetables are cooked but still crisp, about 3 minutes. Return ribs to pan and add soy sauce and coriander. Stir until well combined and ribs have heated through.

SERVES 2

RIGHT: From left: Glazed Pork Ribs with Bell Peppers;
Tofu and Pork Stack with Bean Sauce

Peppered Pork and Omelet Rolls

This dish can be made a day ahead and reheated in the oven before serving. Cover with a lid or foil before reheating so the rolls do not dry out.

3 eggs
2 tablespoons well-flavored chicken stock
2 tablespoons chopped fresh coriander
2 tablespoons oil
10 oz (300g) ground pork
3 cloves garlic, crushed
2 teaspoons purchased or homemade green
    curry paste
5oz (150g) green beans, chopped
1 teaspoon sambal oelek
$^1/_3$ cup ($2^1/_2$fl oz/80ml) coconut cream
$^1/_4$ cup ($^1/_4$oz/7g) chopped mixed fresh coriander
    and basil
6 large bok choy or choy sum leaves
sweet chili sauce (optional)

Beat eggs, stock and coriander in bowl until well combined. Heat lightly oiled 8in (20cm) omelet pan and add enough of egg mixture to coat bottom (about one-sixth). Cook until omelet is set; remove from pan. Repeat with remaining egg mixture to make 6 omelets.

Heat oil in frying pan. Add pork, garlic, curry paste, beans and sambal oelek and cook, stirring occasionally, until pork is cooked and beans are almost tender. Add coconut cream and herbs and simmer about 1 minute or until thick, then remove from heat.

Add bok choy leaves to pan of boiling water and simmer until just wilted. Drain and rinse under cold water. Drain well on paper towels.

Spread a leaf over each omelet, spoon pork mixture onto leaves and roll up omelets.

Place rolls in greased baking dish, cover with foil and bake in 350°F (180°C) oven until heated through, about 15 minutes. Serve rolls with sweet chili sauce.

SERVES 2 TO 4

Spiced Pork Curry

Massaman curry paste is available from Asian food stores. It adds a special flavor to this curry. Serve it with rice or noodles.

2 tablespoons oil
12oz (375g) pork tenderloin, sliced
1 small onion, finely chopped
2 tablespoons massaman curry paste
2 medium potatoes, cubed
$1^1/_2$ cups (12fl oz/375ml) well-flavored
    chicken stock
$^1/_4$ cup (2fl oz/60ml) coconut cream
2 teaspoons fish sauce
2 tablespoons chopped roasted unsalted peanuts
2 tablespoons chopped fresh coriander

Heat oil in saucepan, add pork and cook until lightly browned on both sides. Remove pork from pan. Add onion to pan and cook until soft. Add curry paste and cook several seconds.

Add potatoes, stock, coconut cream, fish sauce and peanuts and simmer uncovered until the potato is just cooked, about 15 minutes. Add pork to pan and simmer a few more minutes or until pork is almost cooked through. Stir in coriander and serve.

SERVES 2 TO 4

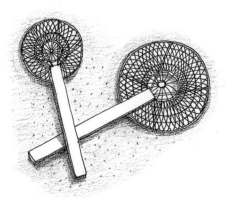

Spicy Pork Ribs

Pork ribs are great to chew on, especially when they have been marinated in a spicy mixture. Use lean ribs for best results.

1¹/₂lb (675g) pork ribs, 3in (8cm) long
2 tablespoons oil
1 tablespoon purchased or homemade red
* curry paste*
2 tablespoons lime juice
1 tablespoon chopped lemongrass
2 teaspoons grated fresh ginger
2 tablespoons chopped fresh coriander

Cut ribs into 4 rib sections. Combine oil, curry paste, lime juice, lemongrass, ginger and coriander in bowl and mix well. Brush rib sections thoroughly with marinade and place in a nonaluminum dish. Cover and refrigerate at least 3 hours or preferably overnight to allow flavors to develop.

Place ribs on rack in roasting pan. Bake in 400°F (200°C) oven, brushing with marinade until browned and cooked through, about 30 minutes.

SERVES 2 TO 4

~ Tip ~

Chop several stalks of lemongrass, grate a large piece of fresh ginger and chop a good handful of fresh coriander. Mix them together and freeze in 2-tablespoon batches to have on hand for a quick marinade addition.

Barbecued Pork with Spinach

This dish is very simple to prepare. Cook it at the last minute and serve with a noodle or rice dish. Remember to increase or decrease the sambal oelek for a hotter or milder chili flavor.

1 tablespoon oil
2 cloves garlic, finely chopped
6¹/₂oz (200g) piece Chinese barbecued pork, sliced
1 bunch fresh spinach, coarsely shredded
2 tablespoons oyster sauce
2 tablespoons well-flavored chicken or
* vegetable stock*
2 teaspoons sambal oelek

Heat oil in wok or large frying pan, add garlic and pork and stir-fry 2 minutes. Add spinach, oyster sauce, stock and sambal oelek and simmer, stirring gently, until spinach is just wilted.

SERVES 2 TO 4

VARIATIONS

- ◆ Use 2 sliced single chicken breast fillets in place of pork.
- ◆ Add 2oz (60g) peeled and deveined cooked shrimp with the spinach.
- ◆ Add 12 quartered stalks of fresh asparagus with spinach.

Stir-Fried Pork with Red Curry Paste

Use a good-quality purchased or a homemade red curry paste (see page 154). You can increase the curry paste for a spicier curry if you like.

13oz (390g) lean diced pork
2 tablespoons oil
1 tablespoon purchased or homemade red
  curry paste
2 kaffir lime leaves, finely shredded, or 1
  teaspoon grated lime zest
2 small zucchini, thinly sliced
1 tablespoon fish sauce
1 tablespoon well-flavored chicken stock
2 tablespoons shredded fresh basil

Remove any fat from pork. Heat oil in wok or large frying pan, add pork and stir-fry until lightly browned.

Add curry paste, lime leaves, zucchini, fish sauce and stock and stir-fry until pork is just cooked through. Stir in basil and serve immediately.

SERVES 2 TO 4

VARIATIONS

◆ Add a good handful of cooked cubed sweet potato for a sweet flavor and delicious texture.
◆ Use half pork and half chicken thigh fillets.

Pork with Citrus Marinade and Spinach

All parts of the coriander plant are used in Thai cooking. Chop the stems with the leaves, as they are full of flavor too. The roots are also used in all types of dishes, such as the marinade in this recipe.

13oz (390g) pork tenderloin
2 coriander roots, finely chopped
1 tablespoon chopped fresh coriander leaves
  and stems
1 tablespoon chopped fresh lemongrass
1 tablespoon sweet chili sauce
1 tablespoon lime juice
1 tablespoon oil
SPINACH
1 bunch fresh spinach
1 tablespoon oil
1 clove garlic, crushed
1 tablespoon sweet chili sauce

Remove any fat from pork. Place pork in nonaluminum dish. Combine coriander roots, leaves and stems, lemongrass, chili sauce, lime juice and oil and pour over pork, turning to coat well. Cover and refrigerate at least 3 hours.

Discard spinach stems. Heat oil in wok or large frying pan. Add garlic and spinach leaves, cover and cook until spinach is wilted. Add chili sauce and stir gently to combine. Keep spinach warm.

Drain pork and broil, panfry or barbecue, brushing with marinade, until just cooked through. Slice pork and serve on bed of spinach.

SERVES 2 TO 4

RIGHT: From top: Stir-Fried Pork with Red Curry Paste; Pork with Citrus Marinade and Spinach

Layered Pork and Mushroom Casserole

1 tablespoon dried shrimp
10oz (300g) boneless pork chops
2 teaspoons oil
1 small carrot, thinly sliced
1 tablespoon chopped fresh ginger
1 teaspoon chopped fresh coriander root
4 green onions, chopped
3½oz (100g) large mushrooms, sliced
1 potato, thinly sliced
1 teaspoon sesame oil
1 teaspoon curry powder
2 cloves garlic, crushed
1 teaspoon fish sauce
½ cup (4fl oz/125ml) water
1 tomato, cut into 10 wedges
chopped fresh coriander (optional)

Cover shrimp with hot water in small bowl and let stand 30 minutes. Drain, then chop finely.

Cut pork into 1¼in (3cm) pieces. Heat oil in wok or medium frying pan until hot. Add pork and stir-fry until browned, then drain on paper towels. Transfer pork to 4 cup (32fl oz/1L) casserole and sprinkle with chopped shrimp. Arrange carrot over top.

Add ginger and coriander root to wok and cook about 1 minute or until aromatic. Add green onions and mushrooms and stir-fry about 3 minutes or until mushrooms are lightly browned. Spoon mushroom mixture over carrot. Arrange potato over mushrooms.

Heat sesame oil in same wok. Add curry powder and garlic and cook 1 minute or until aromatic. Add fish sauce and water and bring to boil; pour over potatoes.

Arrange tomato over potatoes, cover and bake in 350°F (180°C) oven 1 hour. Sprinkle with coriander if desired.

SERVES 2 TO 4

Ginger Pork Steaks with Honey Spiced Onions

The pork is panfried in this dish, but you can barbecue it instead. You may prefer to serve it as a whole steak with the honey glazed onions on the side, a great idea for a barbecue.

1 tablespoon grated fresh ginger
2 cloves garlic, crushed
1 teaspoon freshly ground black pepper
1 teaspoon grated lime zest
2 pork loin medallions
1 tablespoon oil
¼ teaspoon five spice powder
pinch chili powder
2 onions, each cut into 8 wedges
3 green onions, cut into 1½in (4cm) lengths
1 tablespoon honey
2 teaspoons fish sauce
2 tablespoons light soy sauce
1 tablespoon lime juice

Combine ginger, garlic, pepper and lime zest in small bowl. Rub mixture all over pork, cover and refrigerate 1 hour.

Heat oil in frying pan and cook pork until browned all over and just cooked through. Remove from pan, slice into thin strips and keep warm.

Heat same pan and add five spice powder, chili powder, onions and green onions; stir-fry quickly until onion starts to turn bright green. Stir in honey, fish sauce, soy sauce and lime juice. Serve with sliced pork.

SERVES 2

Pork and Bean Sprout Pancakes

The rice flour gives these pancakes a very delicate crispy texture. They are best made in a well seasoned or nonstick frying pan.

2 tablespoons split yellow mung beans
1½ tablespoons rice flour
1½ tablespoons all-purpose flour
¼ teaspoon ground turmeric
1 tablespoon chopped fresh garlic chives
½ cup (4fl oz/125ml) coconut milk
1 egg, lightly beaten
¼ cup (2fl oz/60ml) water, approximately
8oz (250g) pork tenderloin
3 cloves garlic, crushed
1 tablespoon fish sauce
¼ teaspoon freshly ground black pepper
2 tablespoons oil, approximately
1 onion, thinly sliced
2½oz (75g) mushrooms, thinly sliced
½ cup (about 1½oz/40g) bean sprouts

Place mung beans in small saucepan, cover with cold water and bring to boil. Simmer uncovered about 20 minutes or until just tender; drain.

Combine flours, turmeric and chives in bowl. Whisk in coconut milk, egg and enough water to form batter the consistency of cream. Let stand while preparing pork.

Cut pork into very thin slices. Combine pork, garlic, fish sauce and pepper in small bowl. Heat some of the oil in omelet pan or frying pan, preferably nonstick, over high heat. Add pork mixture and onion and stir-fry over high heat until pork changes color and onion begins to soften. Remove from pan.

Reduce heat to medium, stir prepared batter and pour half into pan, swirling to coat bottom. Sprinkle half of cooked mung beans all over pancake. Place half of pork mixture, half of mushrooms and half of bean sprouts over half of pancake. Cover and cook over medium heat until well brown underneath and cooked through, about 5 minutes.

Using spatula, carefully fold pancake in half and slide onto serving plate. Keep warm while preparing second pancake the same way.

SERVES 2

Steamed Pork Patties with Minted Peanut Sauce

8oz (250g) ground pork
3oz (100g) ham, finely chopped
2 cloves garlic, crushed
2 teaspoons grated fresh ginger
1 teaspoon fish sauce
1 egg white
3 green onions, finely chopped
2 tablespoons uncooked long-grain rice
1½ tablespoons toasted sesame seeds
sesame oil
MINTED PEANUT SAUCE
Peanut Sauce (see page 155)
1 tablespoon chopped fresh mint

Combine pork, ham, garlic, ginger, fish sauce, egg white and green onions in a bowl. Using lightly oiled hands, divide mixture into 4 portions and form into patties about 3in (7½cm) in diameter. Roll patties in rice and sesame seeds.

Lightly brush steamer with sesame oil. Place patties in steamer and steam until cooked and rice is puffed and tender, about 20 minutes.

For minted peanut sauce combine peanut sauce and half of mint in small bowl. Sprinkle with remaining mint.

Serve patties with small bowl of minted peanut sauce for each person.

SERVES 2

Warm Salad of Egg and Tofu

Julienned vegetables are made by cutting vegetables into very fine sticks, usually about 2in (5cm) in length.

7oz (200g) firm or hard tofu, cubed
4 green onions, sliced
1 clove garlic, crushed
$1/4$ teaspoon chili powder
1 tablespoon light soy sauce
1 tablespoon lime juice
1 tablespoon oil
$1/2$ a $13^{1}/2oz$ (425g) can mini corn,
  quartered lengthwise
1 celery stalk, julienned
1 small red bell pepper, julienned
2 soft-to medium-boiled eggs, quartered
coriander leaves

Place tofu in nonaluminum dish. Combine green onions, garlic, chili powder, soy sauce and lime juice and pour over tofu. Stir to coat. Cover and refrigerate for a few hours.

Drain tofu, reserving marinade. Heat oil in frying pan, add tofu and brown all over. Remove tofu from pan. Add corn, celery and pepper to pan and cook, stirring, 2 minutes. Add marinade and tofu and simmer for a few seconds.

Place vegetables in serving dish; top with tofu and eggs. Drizzle with any liquid left in pan. Sprinkle with coriander leaves and serve immediately.

SERVES 2 TO 4

Nutty Broccoli and Chili Omelet

This omelet can be cut into cubes and served with drinks or as a vegetarian main course.

8oz (250g) broccoli, chopped
3 eggs
2 teaspoons light soy sauce
1–2 medium-size red chilies, chopped
$1/4$ cup (about 1oz/35g) finely chopped roasted
  cashews or peanuts
3 tablespoons chopped fresh coriander
1 tablespoon oil
2 cloves garlic, crushed
6 green onions, finely chopped

Cook broccoli in pan of boiling water until just tender; drain very well. Combine eggs, soy sauce, chilies, cashews and coriander in bowl. Add broccoli and mix well.

Heat oil in 8in (20cm) omelet pan. Add garlic and green onion and cook gently until onion is soft. Pour in egg mixture and stir well. Cover and cook over low heat until bottom of omelet is set and browned. Finish cooking omelet under hot broiler until set in center. Cut into wedges.

SERVES 2 TO 4

VARIATIONS
- In place of broccoli, use potato, yam or pumpkin.
- Any nuts can be used in place of cashews or peanuts—choose from almonds, pistachios, Brazil nuts or pine nuts.

LEFT: From top: Warm Salad of Egg and Tofu; Nutty Broccoli and Chili Omelet

Barbecued Pineapple with Vegetables

Pineapples are grown in abundance throughout Vietnam, Laos and Cambodia, and often appear in both sweet and savory dishes. Pineapple is superb barbecued with the flavors of lemongrass and fresh mint so characteristic of these countries. Use any variety of vegetables available to you, but don't leave out the pineapple, which makes this dish so different.

8oz (225g) piece fresh pineapple
2 small long baby eggplants
1 large firm tomato
4 spears fresh asparagus
2oz (60g) okra
2 tablespoons fresh mint leaves
1 green chili, seeded and finely chopped
DRESSING
Fish Dipping Sauce (see page 155)
1 tablespoon finely chopped lemongrass
2 teaspoons grated fresh ginger
2 teaspoons bean sauce

Peel but do not core pineapple; cut into 2 thick slices. Halve eggplants lengthwise or if especially large, quarter lengthwise. Cut tomato into 4 thick slices. Cut asparagus into 2in (5cm) lengths. Trim tops of okra if necessary. Add asparagus and okra separately to saucepan of boiling water and boil about 1 minute or until just tender. Drain well.

Heat a greased barbecue grill or griddle until hot. Barbecue sliced pineapple, eggplant and tomato until browned on both sides.

For dressing, combine the fish dipping sauce, lemongrass, ginger and bean sauce in a screw-top jar and shake well.

Arrange pineapple on serving plate with eggplant, tomato, asparagus and okra. Drizzle with dressing and sprinkle with mint leaves and chili.

SERVES 2

Tomatoes Stuffed with Rice and Mushrooms

The filling for these tomatoes can be made several hours ahead, and the tomatoes cooked close to serving time. Be careful when browning the tomatoes not to overheat them or the skins may split.

1 Chinese dried mushroom
2 large firm tomatoes
5 teaspoons oil
1 onion, finely chopped
1/2 teaspoon shrimp paste
1 1/3oz (40g) mushrooms, chopped
1 small zucchini, finely chopped
1 1/2 tablespoons uncooked rice
1 cup (8fl oz/250ml) water, approximately
1 teaspoon fish sauce
1 egg, lightly beaten
1/4 cup (2fl oz/60ml) water
1 tablespoon oyster sauce
2 teaspoons tomato paste
1 tablespoon chopped fresh coriander

Cover mushroom with hot water in small bowl and let stand 30 minutes. Discard stem and chop mushroom finely.

Slice tops off tomatoes; discard. Using teaspoon, carefully scrape out pulp. Mash the pulp finely and reserve for sauce.

Heat 3 teaspoons oil in wok or frying pan. Add onion, shrimp paste and mushrooms and stir-fry until soft. Add zucchini and rice and stir-fry 2 minutes. Add 1 cup water, fish sauce and soaked dried mushroom and simmer, uncovered, until the rice is tender and all the liquid has evaporated, about 15 minutes, adding more water during cooking if necessary. Cool slightly, then stir in egg. Spoon rice mixture into prepared tomatoes, pressing firmly.

Heat remaining 2 teaspoons oil. Add tomatoes, browning tops first, then carefully turning to brown bottoms. Add reserved mashed tomato pulp to wok with ¼ cup water, oyster sauce and tomato paste; bring to boil. Simmer covered until the tomatoes are just cooked and the filling has heated through, about 8 minutes. Sprinkle with chopped coriander.

SERVES 2

~ Tip ~

Use a very small teaspoon to remove the pulp from the tomatoes. If the tomatoes are too ripe, the skins may split easily; choose ones that are only just ripe.

Vegetable, Bean Sprout and Egg Strip Stir-Fry

It is best to use fresh bean sprouts in this recipe. They are available from produce markets and Asian food stores. Canned bean sprouts are also available but are not as crisp as the fresh variety.

½ teaspoon sesame oil
1 egg, lightly beaten
1 teaspoon fish sauce
2 teaspoons chopped fresh garlic chives
1 tablespoon oil
4 shallots, peeled and halved
3½oz (100g) green beans, cut diagonally into
    1¼in (3cm) lengths
1 small carrot, thinly sliced
7oz (200g) broccoli, cut into small florets
1 cup (2½oz/80g) bean sprouts
1 tablespoon light soy sauce
1 tablespoon bean sauce
½ cup (4fl oz/125ml) water
sweet chili sauce

Heat sesame oil in frying pan. Combine egg, fish sauce and chives and pour into pan, tilting to form thin omelet. Cook until just set. Remove from pan, roll up and cut into slices ¼in (6mm) wide.

Heat oil in wok or large frying pan. Add shallots, beans and carrot and stir-fry 1 minute. Add broccoli and stir-fry 2 minutes. Add bean sprouts, soy sauce, bean sauce and water and bring to boil; cover and cook 2 minutes. Serve stir-fry topped with egg strips, accompanying each serving with bowl of chili sauce.

SERVES 2

Potato and Artichoke Cakes

4 bottled artichoke hearts, drained well
 and quartered
2 teaspoons fish sauce
2 cloves garlic, crushed
$\frac{1}{2}$ teaspoon freshly ground black pepper
$\frac{1}{2}$ cup (2oz/60g) self-rising flour, sifted
$\frac{1}{4}$ teaspoon ground turmeric
$\frac{1}{3}$ cup (2$\frac{1}{2}$fl oz/80ml) water, approximately
1 small potato (4oz/125g), grated
1 small sweet potato (4oz/125g), grated
3 green onions, sliced
2 tablespoons oil
assorted lettuce leaves, torn
2 tablespoons fresh mint leaves
Fish Dipping Sauce (see page 155)

Combine artichokes, 1 teaspoon fish sauce, garlic and $\frac{1}{4}$ teaspoon of pepper in small bowl.

Combine remaining pepper, flour and turmeric in separate bowl. Whisk in remaining fish sauce and enough water to form batter with consistency of whipping cream. Add potatoes and green onion, mix well.

Heat some of oil in frying pan. Drop one-quarter of mixture into pan and spread into circle about 5in (12$\frac{1}{2}$cm) in diameter. Press 4 pieces of artichoke into cake and cook over medium heat until browned underneath. Turn and cook until other side is browned and cake is cooked through. Drain on paper towels; keep warm. Repeat with remaining potato mixture and artichokes, adding more oil to pan as necessary.

Spread lettuce and mint leaves over platter. Halve or quarter cakes and arrange on greens. Drizzle with fish dipping sauce before serving.

MAKES 4 CAKES

Braised Quail Eggs and Vegetables

If quail eggs are hard to find, use 5 small chicken eggs and boil them for 5 minutes.

10 quail eggs
2 teaspoons sesame oil
2 cloves garlic, crushed
1 onion, chopped
2oz (60g) button mushrooms, halved
1 ripe tomato, chopped
2 teaspoons bean sauce
1 tablespoon fish sauce
$\frac{3}{4}$ cup (6fl oz/185ml) water
1 tablespoon tomato paste
1 carrot, chopped
5oz (150g) pumpkin or rutabaga, chopped

Place eggs in small saucepan and cover with cold water. Bring to boil, then simmer 4 minutes, stirring gently to center yolks. Drain eggs, rinse under cold water and remove shells.

Heat sesame oil in wok or frying pan. Add garlic and onion and stir-fry 1 minute. Add mushrooms and tomato and stir-fry 2 minutes or until tomato is soft. Add quail eggs, bean sauce, fish sauce and combined water and tomato paste. Cover and simmer for 10 minutes. Add carrot and pumpkin and simmer, covered, 20 more minutes or until vegetables are tender.

SERVES 2 TO 4

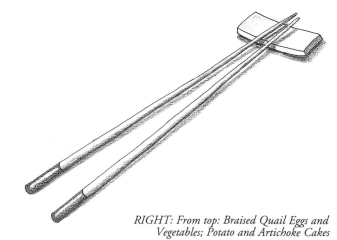

RIGHT: From top: Braised Quail Eggs and
Vegetables; Potato and Artichoke Cakes

Tofu and Vegetable Fresh Spring Rolls with Spicy Dressing

The rice paper holds up well in these fresh-tasting spring rolls. They can be made ahead of time; cover well with plastic wrap and refrigerate until ready to serve.

1 bunch fresh spinach

1 carrot, julienned

2 green onions, cut into 3in (8cm) strips

10 rice paper sheets, 7in (18cm) square

5oz (150g) firm or hard tofu, cut into strips 3in (8cm) thin

10 long mint leaves

SPICY DRESSING

2 tablespoons white vinegar

2 teaspoons sugar

1 tablespoon sweet chili sauce

2 tablespoons lime juice

1 clove garlic, crushed

$^1/_4$ teaspoon sesame oil

2 teaspoons chopped fresh coriander

Discard spinach stems and place leaves in saucepan. Cover and cook spinach gently until wilted; drain well and cool. Squeeze any excess liquid from cooled spinach.

Drop carrot into saucepan of boiling water and boil until tender; drain well. Drop green onion into boiling water for 30 seconds or until softened; drain well.

For dressing, combine all ingredients in bowl and mix well.

Soak 1 sheet of rice paper in warm water just until softened. Place on board. Top with some of the spinach, carrot, green onion, tofu and 1 mint leaf. Drizzle with a little dressing and roll up firmly, folding in sides. Repeat with remaining rice paper, vegetables, tofu, mint and some of the dressing. Serve spring rolls with remaining dressing.

MAKES 10

Top rice paper with spinach, carrot, green onion, tofu and mint.

Roll up firmly, folding in sides.

RIGHT: Tofu and Vegetable Fresh Spring Rolls with Spicy Dressing

Eggplant and Potato Curry

You can use regular or sweet potato in this curry. Other root vegetables such as rutabaga, yam or celeriac can be used in place of the potato.

1 tablespoon oil
1 small onion, chopped
2 cloves garlic, crushed
2 tablespoons chopped lemongrass
1–2 medium-size red chilies, chopped
2 teaspoons grated fresh ginger
2 tablespoons chopped fresh coriander
6 long baby eggplants, sliced
6 small new potatoes, halved
$^{1}/_{4}$ cup (1oz/30g) green peas
$^{3}/_{4}$ cup (6fl oz/185ml) well-flavored vegetable stock
$^{1}/_{2}$ cup (4fl oz/125ml) coconut milk

Combine oil, onion, garlic, lemongrass, chilies, ginger and coriander in food processor and grind to paste. Transfer paste to saucepan and cook gently several minutes.

Add eggplant, potatoes, peas, stock and coconut milk and simmer covered, until vegetables are tender, about 15 minutes.

SERVES 2 TO 4

VARIATIONS

◆ If long baby eggplants are not available, use a chopped large eggplant.
◆ For a richer, creamier curry, use coconut cream in place of coconut milk.

Marinated Tofu with Vegetables

Use the firmest tofu you can find; it is ideal for marinating and frying. The texture of "firm" or "hard" tofu is quite meaty and provides a substantial vegetarian meal.

8oz (250g) firm or hard tofu
2 cloves garlic, crushed
1 tablespoon light soy sauce
1 tablespoon oyster sauce
2 tablespoons oil
2 teaspoons sesame seeds
1 small onion, thinly sliced
2oz (60g) green beans, sliced
$^{1}/_{2}$ red bell pepper, chopped
$^{1}/_{2}$ cup ($^{1}/_{2}$oz/15g) small mint leaves

Cut tofu into slices $^{1}/_{2}$in (1cm) thick and then place in nonaluminum dish. Combine garlic, sauces, half of oil and sesame seeds and pour over tofu, turning tofu to coat. Cover and refrigerate several hours to allow flavors to develop.

Drain tofu, reserving marinade. Heat remaining oil in frying pan. Add tofu and cook until browned on both sides. Remove tofu from frying pan.

Add onion, beans and bell pepper to pan and stir-fry until partially cooked. Stir in marinade and add tofu; simmer until heated through. Add mint leaves and serve immediately.

SERVES 2 TO 4

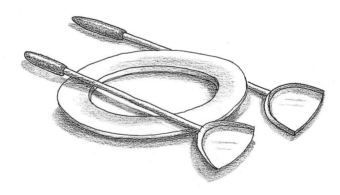

Rice Noodle, Peanut and Spinach Stir-Fry

Use any of your favorite nuts in this stir-fry, or try a mixture. For a strict vegetarian dish, you will have to use homemade red curry paste, omitting the shrimp paste when making it.

8 Chinese dried mushrooms
7oz (200g) dried rice stick noodles
1 bunch fresh spinach
2 tablespoons oil
3–4 teaspoons purchased or homemade
  red curry paste
1 clove garlic, crushed
1/4 cup (2fl oz/60ml) well-flavored vegetable stock
1/4 cup (about 1oz/35g) finely chopped roasted
  peanuts
1/2 teaspoon sesame oil

Place mushrooms in bowl and cover with hot water; soak 20 minutes. Drain and squeeze out any excess liquid. Cut mushrooms into thin slices, discarding tough stems.

Place noodles in heatproof bowl and cover with boiling water. Let stand 10 minutes. Drain noodles, tossing through a little oil to keep from sticking together.

Halve spinach leaves and discard stems. Heat oil in wok or large frying pan. Add curry paste and garlic and cook gently for a few seconds. Add mushrooms, spinach and stock and stir gently until spinach is just wilted. Add the noodles, peanuts and sesame oil and toss gently until heated through.

SERVES 2 TO 4

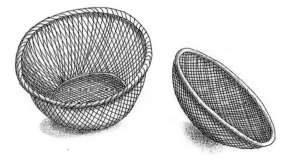

Chickpeas and Couscous with Herbs and Coconut Cream

Couscous is a type of fine pasta made from semolina. It does not need cooking, just a soak in boiling liquid.

1/2 cup (3oz/90g) couscous
1/2 cup (4fl oz/125ml) well-flavored
  vegetable stock
1 tablespoon oil
2 cloves garlic, crushed
6 green onions, chopped
2 teaspoons purchased or homemade red
  curry paste
10oz (310g) can chickpeas, drained
2 tablespoons chopped fresh coriander
1 tablespoon chopped lemongrass
1/3 cup (2 1/2fl oz/80ml) coconut cream

Place couscous in heatproof bowl. Bring stock to boil in saucepan, pour over couscous and mix well. Let stand 10 minutes or until stock is completely absorbed.

Heat oil in wok or large frying pan. Add garlic, green onion and curry paste and cook gently 1 minute. Add chickpeas, coriander, lemongrass and coconut cream and stir until heated through. Add couscous and toss gently with a fork until combined. Serve warm or at room temperature.

SERVES 2 TO 4

VARIATION
Substitute 3 1/2oz (100g) dried rice stick noodles for couscous. Prepare noodles as in Rice Noodle, Peanut and Spinach Stir-Fry (at left), using stock as part of soaking liquid.

Cinnamon Sausage Baguette

The sausage can also be eaten cold or sliced, barbecued and served with a dipping sauce.

1 baguette, halved
Peanut Sauce (see page 155)
½ teaspoon sesame oil
1 tablespoon toasted sesame seeds
Pickled Carrot or Cucumber
   (see page 129)
assorted lettuces such as oakleaf, butter or
   romaine lettuce
1 cup (2½oz/80g) bean sprouts
¼ cup (¼oz/7g) fresh mint leaves
2 tablespoons fresh coriander leaves
CINNAMON SAUSAGE
1 tablespoon dried shrimp
¼ cup (about 1oz/35g) couscous
¼ cup (2fl oz/60ml) boiling chicken stock
   or water
7oz (200g) ground pork
1 tablespoon fish sauce
4 cloves garlic, crushed
½ teaspoon freshly ground black pepper
6 green onions, finely chopped
1 teaspoon cinnamon
1 tablespoon sesame seeds, toasted

Split each baguette half lengthwise without cutting completely through. Combine peanut sauce with sesame oil and sesame seeds in small bowl. Spread some of mixture onto each side of split baguette.

To make cinnamon sausage, cover shrimp with hot water in small bowl and let stand 30 minutes. Drain and chop finely. Combine couscous and stock in small bowl and let stand 5 minutes or until all liquid has been absorbed.

Combine shrimp, pork, fish sauce, garlic, pepper, green onion and cinnamon in food processor and blend until smooth. Stir in couscous. With lightly wet hands, mold mixture into sausage shape about 2in (5cm) in diameter. Roll in sesame seeds until completely coated. Place sausage onto 13in (33cm)

square of baking parchment or lightly greased waxed paper, roll up tightly and twist ends.

Place sausage in steamer and steam 20 minutes. Let stand 5 minutes before unwrapping. Let cool slightly before slicing.

Place sliced cinnamon sausage, pickled carrot or cucumber, lettuce leaves, bean sprouts, mint and coriander leaves into split baguette and spoon more peanut sauce mixture over before serving.

SERVES 4

Crisp Tofu in Tomato Sauce

Serve with steamed rice.

7oz (200g) firm tofu
1 tablespoon oil
4 green onions, chopped
3 cloves garlic, crushed
3 ripe tomatoes, chopped
1 teaspoon fish sauce
1 tablespoon lime juice
¼ cup (2fl oz/60ml) water
2 teaspoons tomato paste
2 tablespoons chopped fresh coriander

Drain tofu well; pat dry with paper towels. Cut into 1¼in (3cm) pieces. Brush all over with some of oil, and place on baking sheet. Broil only until lightly browned, turn pieces to brown both sides.

Heat remaining oil in wok or saucepan. Add green onion and garlic and stir over medium heat until onion is soft. Add tomatoes and cook, stirring, until the tomatoes are soft, about 3 minutes. Add fish sauce, lime juice and combined water and tomato paste and bring to boil, then simmer uncovered 2 minutes. Add tofu to wok with coriander and stir until heated through.

SERVES 2 TO 4

LEFT: Crisp Tofu in Tomato Sauce

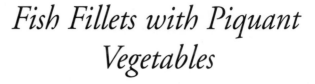

Steamed Whole Fish with Lemongrass and Chili

1 lime
1lb (450g) whole snapper or 2 10oz (300g)
  snappers, scaled and gutted
2 stems lemongrass, halved lengthwise
1 slice lime, halved
2 teaspoons grated fresh ginger
2 teaspoons fish sauce
2 teaspoons oyster sauce
1 tablespoon lime juice
1 teaspoon sesame oil
2 cloves garlic, crushed
1 onion, sliced
1 red chili, sliced
2 green onions, sliced

Using vegetable peeler and avoiding white pith, peel rind from lime, then cut into thin strips.

Make 3 deep cuts in each side of fish. Place lemongrass, lime slices and ginger into cavity of the fish and secure cavity with toothpicks. Place fish on large plate that will fit in steamer. (If you have a small steamer, buy 2 small fish instead.)

Combine fish sauce, oyster sauce, lime juice, sesame oil and garlic in small bowl. Brush mixture all over fish. Sprinkle with onion. Place fish (on plate) in steamer and steam 10 minutes. Sprinkle with lime rind, chili and green onion, cover and steam 10 more minutes or until fish is cooked through, spooning any liquid accumulating in the plate over fish during cooking.

SERVES 2

Fish Fillets with Piquant Vegetables

3 green onions
6 baby carrots or 3 small carrots
3 spring (bulb) onions
1 long red chili
3 tablespoons oil
2 cloves garlic, sliced
1 tablespoon tamarind puree
2 tablespoons lime juice
2 tablespoons fish sauce
1 teaspoon sugar
2 cod fillets
2 tablespoons cornstarch
1/2 teaspoon freshly ground black pepper
Steamed Rice (see page 49; optional)

Cut green onions into 1¼in (3cm) lengths. Cut baby carrots and spring (bulb) onions in half lengthwise; cut small carrots into quarters lengthwise. Halve red chili lengthwise, remove seeds and cut into long thin strips.

Heat 1 tablespoon oil in medium saucepan. Add green shallots, spring onion and garlic and stir over high heat until onions are just browned; remove from pan. To same pan add carrots, chili, tamarind puree, lime juice, fish sauce and sugar. Bring to boil, then simmer uncovered until liquid has reduced and thickened. Return onion mixture to pan and stir well; keep warm while cooking fish.

Pat fish dry with paper towels. Coat in cornstarch seasoned with pepper.

Heat remaining 2 tablespoons oil in frying pan large enough to hold both fish fillets. Cook fish until well browned on both sides and just cooked through, about 6 minutes. Serve topped with vegetable mixture, accompanied by bowl of steamed rice if desired.

SERVES 2

RIGHT: Steamed Whole Fish with Lemongrass and Chili

Grilled Fish Fillets with Thai Pesto

The pesto can be made a week ahead or frozen for several weeks. *Pesto* is an Italian word meaning ground or crushed. This is a Thai-flavored variation of the famous Italian pesto sauce. This quantity of pesto will make 4 servings.

1 clove garlic, crushed
1 tablespoon oil
2–4 white fish fillets
THAI PESTO
3oz (90g) bunch fresh coriander with roots
$^1/_2$oz/15g ($^1/_2$ cup) basil leaves
2 tablespoons chopped lemongrass
2 cloves garlic, crushed
2 teaspoons fish sauce
1 tablespoon lime juice
$^1/_4$ cup (2fl oz/60ml) oil
1 tablespoon sweet chili sauce

To make pesto, coarsely chop coriander leaves, stems and roots in processor. Add basil, lemongrass, garlic, fish sauce and lime juice and chop finely. With machine running, add oil and chili sauce and process to paste consistency.

Combine garlic and oil with 2 tablespoons pesto. Grill fish, brushing with garlic, oil and pesto mixture, until cooked through. Serve fish topped with generous dollop of remaining pesto. Place any remaining pesto in clean jar, top with layer of oil and refrigerate for up to 1 week.

SERVES 2 TO 4

Baked Whole Fish

I generally use snapper in this recipe, but any white fish can be used.

2 whole fish (13oz/400g each), gutted and scaled
1in (2.5cm) piece fresh ginger, finely shredded
2 cloves garlic, thinly sliced
$^1/_4$ red bell pepper, thinly sliced
1 medium red chili, thinly sliced
$1^1/_2$ tablespoons white vinegar
1 teaspoon sugar
1 tablespoon oil
coriander leaves
CHILI SAUCE
1–2 medium-size red chilies
2 cloves garlic, finely chopped
1 tablespoon sugar
2 tablespoons lime juice
2 teaspoons finely chopped roasted cashews

Make deep cuts, about $^3/_4$in (2cm) apart, along both sides of fish. Place in greased baking dish. Combine the ginger, garlic, bell pepper, chili, vinegar, sugar and oil in bowl. Spoon mixture inside fish and over top. Sprinkle with coriander leaves.

Cover and bake in 350°F (180°C) oven until the fish flakes easily with a fork, about 20 minutes.

While fish is cooking, make chili sauce by combining all ingredients in bowl and mixing well. Serve fish with Chili Sauce.

SERVES 2 TO 4

LEFT: Grilled Fish Fillets with Thai Pesto

Curried Shrimp with Cucumber and Asparagus

This is a very quick curry that is best made close to serving time. If you have time, make the curry paste an hour ahead. Combine the shrimp with about 1 tablespoon of the curry paste; cover and refrigerate for 1 hour. Serve curry with bowl of steamed rice or crusty bread.

1 clove garlic, crushed
1 small onion, grated
1 tablespoon chopped lemongrass
1/2 teaspoon ground turmeric
1 teaspoon paprika
pinch allspice
1 teaspoon chili powder
1/4 teaspoon cinnamon
1 teaspoon ground coriander
pinch powdered saffron
2 teaspoons brown sugar
1 tablespoon lime juice
1 small cucumber
12 spears fresh asparagus
12 medium uncooked shrimp
1 tablespoon oil
2/3 cup (5 1/2 fl oz/165ml) water
2 teaspoons fish sauce
1 teaspoon cornstarch
1/2 cup (4fl oz/125ml) coconut cream
fresh coriander sprigs

For curry paste, combine garlic, onion, lemongrass, turmeric, paprika, allspice, chili powder, cinnamon, coriander, saffron, sugar and lime juice in mortar or blender and grind to paste.

Halve cucumber lengthwise and scape out the seeds with a teaspoon. Cut cucumber into 1/4in (5mm) slices and asparagus into 1 1/4in (3cm)) lengths. Peel and devein shrimp, leaving tails intact.

Heat oil in wok or medium saucepan. Combine water, fish sauce and cornstarch. Add curry paste to wok and cook, stirring, until bubbling and aromatic,

about 2 minutes. Add shrimp and stir until well coated. Add cucumber and asparagus, then cornstarch mixture and coconut cream. Bring to boil, stirring; simmer uncovered until the shrimp are cooked and sauce is thickened, about 3 minutes.

Serve curry garnished with coriander sprigs.

SERVES 2

Broiled Crab and Shrimp Cakes

A healthy alternative to the traditionally deep-fried seafood cakes, these can be eaten hot or cold. You may like to serve them as appetizers – cut into quarters.

3 1/2 oz (100g) crabmeat
4 cloves garlic, crushed
4 green onions, finely chopped
1 tablespoon chopped fresh dill
1/2 teaspoon freshly ground black pepper
2 anchovy fillets, finely chopped
13oz (400g) medium uncooked shrimp, peeled and deveined
1 tablespoon oil or Shallot Oil (see page 155)
Fish Dipping Sauce (see page 155)
1 tablespoon tamarind puree

Combine crabmeat, garlic, green onion, dill, pepper and anchovy fillets in food processor and chop very finely. Add shrimp and process until mixture forms thick paste. Divide evenly into 6 portions.

With lightly oiled hands, mold each portion into a 2 1/2 in (6cm) patty. Arrange patties on lightly oiled broiler pan and brush with oil. Broil until browned and cooked through, about 5 minutes on both sides. Combine fish dipping sauce and tamarind puree and serve with cakes.

SERVES 2

RIGHT: Curried Shrimp with Cucumber and Asparagus

Wooden spoon from Corso del Fiori; wood spice box from Orson & Blake

Wood measure from Orson & Blake; wooden stove and tin platter from Corso del Fiori

Pork Noodle and Stuffed Squid

4 small or 2 medium cleaned squid
2 tablespoons oil
1 tablespoon fish sauce
Fish Dipping Sauce (see page 155)
2oz (50g) radish, grated
FILLING
2 Chinese dried mushrooms
1 tablespoon dried shrimp
$\frac{1}{3}$oz (10g) rice vermicelli
$2\frac{1}{2}$oz (75g) ground pork
2 green onions, finely chopped
2 cloves garlic, crushed
2 teaspoons grated fresh ginger
1 egg white
1 tablespoon rice vinegar
1 teaspoon light soy sauce
1 tablespoon chopped fresh mint

To make filling, cover mushrooms with hot water in bowl and let stand 30 minutes. Drain. Remove and discard stems; chop mushrooms finely. Cover shrimp with hot water in small bowl and let stand 30 minutes. Drain and chop finely. Cover rice vermicelli with boiling water in small bowl and let stand 30 minutes. Drain and cut into short lengths with scissors.

Combine mushrooms, shrimp, vermicelli, pork, green onions, garlic, ginger, egg white, vinegar, soy sauce and mint in bowl.

Spoon filling into squid until about two-thirds full. (Squid shrink during cooking, so avoid overfilling.) Secure openings with toothpicks. Prick each squid twice so excess liquid can be released.

Heat oil in wok or medium saucepan and lightly brown squid all over. Reduce heat to medium, cover and cook squid 12 minutes, turning to brown evenly.

Remove from heat, add fish sauce and turn squid to coat with pan juices. Remove toothpicks and slice squid. Serve with small bowl of fish dipping sauce mixed with radish for each person.

SERVES 2

Stir-Fried Octopus with Pickled Mustard Greens

10oz (300g) pickled mustard greens, drained
1lb (450g) baby octopus
2 cloves garlic, crushed
$\frac{1}{2}$ teaspoon freshly ground black pepper
1 tablespoon fish sauce
1 tablespoon oil
$\frac{1}{2}$ small fennel bulb, thinly sliced
1 onion, sliced
2 teaspoons brown sugar
1 tablespoon rice vinegar
2 green onions
1 medium tomato, seeded and sliced
1 small red chili, finely chopped
fresh fennel sprigs

Place mustard greens in bowl and cover with water. Let stand overnight. Drain well and cut into smaller pieces.

Remove heads and black beaks from octopus and discard. (Beak is at center of body where legs meet.) Combine octopus, garlic, pepper and fish sauce in bowl, cover and let stand for 30 minutes.

Heat oil in wok or frying pan, add fennel and onion and stir-fry 2 minutes. Add octopus mixture and stir-fry over high heat or until the octopus is tender, about 4 minutes. Add sugar, vinegar, pickled mustard, green onions and tomato and stir until heated through. Serve sprinkled with chili and fennel fennel.

SERVES 2

LEFT: From left: Pork and Noodle Stuffed Squid; Stir-Fried Octopus with Pickled Mustard Greens

Shrimp with Lemongrass and Chili

Fresh kaffir lime leaves are available from Asian food stores. If you prefer, you can used dried leaves. Soak them in hot water for several hours before shredding them. The leaves add a lovely, subtle lime flavor to this dish.

1lb (450g) large uncooked shrimp
1 tablespoon oil
1 teaspoon purchased or homemade green
*   curry paste*
2 tablespoons thinly sliced lemongrass
1–2 medium-size red chilies, chopped
1 tablespoon fish sauce
3 kaffir lime leaves, shredded, or 1 teaspoon
*   grated lime zest*
1 teaspoon sugar
2 tablespoons coconut milk

Peel and devein shrimp, leaving tails intact. Heat oil in wok or large frying pan. Add curry paste and cook a few seconds.

Add shrimp, lemongrass, chilies, fish sauce, lime leaves, sugar and coconut milk. Simmer gently, stirring occasionally, until shrimp are just cooked through.

SERVES 2 TO 4

VARIATIONS

◆ Substitute 8oz (250g) cubed firm white fish fillets for half of shrimp.

◆ Add 5oz (150g) snow peas with shrimp.

Grilled Octopus

The marinade in this recipe can also be used with shrimp, fish cubes or squid. It is best to allow the octopus to marinate overnight; this not only improves the flavor but also tenderizes the octopus deliciously.

1lb (450g) baby octopus
1 tablespoon light soy sauce
1 tablespoon oil
1 tablespoon dry sherry
2 cloves garlic, crushed
1 teaspoon grated lime zest
2 tablespoons lime juice
2 medium-size red chilies, chopped
2 tablespoons chopped fresh coriander

Prepare octopus by cutting away heads from just below eyes. Cut octopus in half. Remove black beak at center of body where legs meet.

Combine soy sauce, oil, sherry, garlic, lime zest and juice, chilies and coriander in bowl. Add octopus and mix thoroughly. Cover and refrigerate several hours or preferably overnight to allow flavors to develop.

Drain octopus and cook on stovetop grill or barbecue until just cooked through. If you like, bring any remaining marinade to boil in saucepan and serve with octopus as sauce.

SERVES 2 TO 4

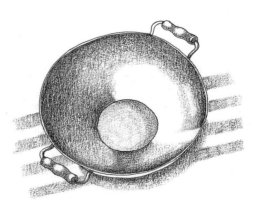

RIGHT: From top: Shrimp with Lemongrass and Chili; Grilled Octopus

Seafood with Herbs, Chili and Garlic

1 small uncooked crab
6 medium uncooked shrimp
6 small black mussels
2 tablespoons oil
7oz (200g) firm white fish fillet, cut into
*   1in (2.5cm) cubes*
3 small cleaned squid, sliced into rings
1 tablespoon purchased or homemade red
*   curry paste*
2 fresh coriander roots, finely chopped
2 cloves garlic, finely chopped
1 tablespoon chopped lemongrass
1–2 small red chilies, thinly sliced
2 tablespoons fish sauce
1 tablespoon oyster sauce
1/2 cup (4fl oz/125ml) water
1 cup (1oz/30g) chopped mixed fresh basil,
*   coriander and mint*
4 green onions, cut into short lengths

To prepare crab, slide strong knife under top body shell from back; lever off shell. Scrape away white gills along sides. Wash well. Using sharp knife, cut body into quarters. Remove large claws and crack with nutcracker along length (or tap gently along claws with meat mallet).

Peel and devein shrimp, leaving tails intact. Scrub mussels. Pull away fibrous beards and scrape away any seaweed on shells.

Heat half of oil in large wok or frying pan. Add enough fish cubes to cover bottom and cook through. Transfer fish to bowl. Repeat with remaining fish. Add squid rings to wok and stir-fry until they are just cooked, about 1 minute. Add to fish. Wipe out wok with paper towel.

Heat remaining oil in wok. Add curry paste, coriander roots, garlic, lemongrass and half of chili. Cook 1 minute, then stir in sauces and water.

Add crab, shrimp and mussels to wok, making sure thick pieces of crab and the mussels are on bottom and submerged in liquid. Cover wok and simmer until mussels open and crab is cooked through, about 5 minutes. Gently stir in fish cubes, squid, herbs and green onion, toss gently until heated through. Sprinkle with remaining chili before serving.

SERVES 2 TO 4

Baked Noodles with Shrimp and Broccoli

3¹/2oz (100g) dried rice stick noodles
1 tablespoon oil
1 small onion, thinly sliced
2 cloves garlic, crushed
12 uncooked jumbo shrimp, peeled and deveined
2 teaspoons grated fresh ginger
1 tablespoon chopped lemongrass
1 medium-size red chili, finely chopped
2 tablespoons chopped fresh coriander
2 teaspoons oyster sauce
2 teaspoons light soy sauce
1/4 teaspoon sesame oil
3¹/2oz (100g) broccoli, cut into small florets
2 tablespoons well-flavored chicken stock

Place noodles in heatproof bowl and cover with boiling water. Let stand 5 minutes, then drain well.

Heat oil in saucepan. Add onion and garlic and cook gently until onion is very soft and lightly browned. Remove from heat and stir in noodles and all remaining ingredients. Mix very well.

Divide mixture between two 2 cup (16fl oz/500ml) baking dishes. Cover and bake in 350°F (180°C) oven until shrimp are cooked through, about 25 minutes. Serve in baking dishes.

SERVES 2

RIGHT: Seafood with Herbs, Chili and Garlic

Stone dish from Orson & Blake; cane basket from Corso del Fiori

Lamb Rolls with Sesame Peanut Sauce

These rolls also look attractive served as an appetizer for 4 people. They can be made several hours ahead and kept covered in the refrigerator.

1¼in (3cm) piece fresh ginger
½ large avocado, sliced
2 tablespoons lime juice
1 tablespoon oil
11 oz (330g) lamb fillets
1 tablespoon dry sherry
1 tablespoon fish sauce
5oz (150g) daikon radish, julienned
2½oz (75g) thinly sliced ham, julienned
1 small carrot, julienned
⅓ cup (⅓oz/10g) fresh mint leaves
4 round sheets rice paper (banh trang),
    8½in (22cm) in diameter

SESAME PEANUT SAUCE

Peanut Sauce (see page 155)
1 tablespoon sesame seeds, toasted
½ teaspoon sesame oil

Cut ginger into thin strips. Combine avocado and lime juice in bowl. Heat oil in frying pan. Add lamb and cook, turning, until well browned and just cooked, about 8 minutes. Add sherry and fish sauce, and allow mixture to bubble. Remove from heat, then cool. Cut lamb into 8 long strips and drizzle with pan juices.

Have fillings prepared in order of use to help with quick wrapping of rolls: first avocado, then lamb, radish, ham, carrot, ginger and mint leaves.

Soak 1 sheet of rice paper in bowl of warm water for about 30 seconds until soft and pliable. Place on board. Place ¼ of avocado, lamb strips, radish, ham strips, carrot strips, ginger and mint leaves along center of rice paper. Roll up rice paper quickly and tightly to enclose filling. Repeat with remaining sheets of rice paper and fillings.

For sesame peanut sauce, combine peanut sauce with half of seeds and sesame oil in a small bowl. Divide sauce between individual bowls and sprinkle with remaining sesame seeds.

Serve rolls whole or cut diagonally in half. Accompany with sesame peanut sauce.

SERVES 2

Place fillings onto softened rice paper.

Roll up rice paper quickly and tightly.

LEFT: Lamb Rolls with Sesame Peanut Sauce

Fish Strips and Shrimp with Ginger and Herbs

Choose a firm fish fillet that will hold together when cooked. If you really enjoy the flavor of ginger, add twice the amount.

10oz (300g) boneless white fish fillet, cut into
* 2in (5cm) strips*
6 uncooked jumbo shrimp, peeled and deveined
2 tablespoons lime juice
2 teaspoons grated fresh ginger
2 coriander roots, finely chopped
2 tablespoons chopped fresh coriander leaves
1 tablespoon chopped fresh basil leaves
2 teaspoons fish sauce
1 tablespoon oil
steamed rice or noodles

Place fish and shrimp in nonaluminum dish. Combine lime juice, ginger, coriander roots and leaves, basil, fish sauce and oil, pour over seafood and mix thoroughly. Cover and refrigerate at least 2 hours to allow flavors to develop. Transfer fish mixture to wok or large frying pan and simmer, stirring occasionally, until the fish and shrimp are just cooked through, about 5 minutes. Serve with steamed rice or noodles.

SERVES 2 TO 4

Creamy Beef Curry

I use round steak in this recipe, but you can use any tender cut of beef, such as boneless sirloin, fillet or rib eye.

10oz (300g) tender cut of beef
1 tablespoon oil
1 tablespoon purchased or homemade green
* curry paste*
1 cup (8fl oz/250ml) coconut milk
2 teaspoons fish sauce
1 teaspoon sugar
1/2 14oz (425g) can mini corn
1/3 cup (2oz/60g) canned straw mushrooms,
* drained*
1/2 cup (1/2oz/15g) small basil leaves
Steamed Rice (see page 49)

Cut beef into thin slices, discarding any fat. Heat oil in wok or large frying pan, add beef and stir-fry over high heat until browned. Remove beef from wok.

Add curry paste to wok and cook gently for a few seconds. Add coconut milk, fish sauce, sugar, corn and mushrooms and bring to boil; simmer for 5 minutes. Add beef and basil and simmer, until beef is heated through, about 2 minutes. Serve with steamed rice.

SERVES 2 TO 4

> ~ *Tip* ~
> To cut meat into thin slices, wrap it in plastic or freezer wrap in a single layer and partially freeze. Remove meat from wrap and cut into thin slices while partially frozen using a sharp knife.

Roast Lamb with Thai Seasoning

Ask the butcher to bone the leg of lamb for you.

3lb (1.5kg) leg of lamb, boned
³/₄ cup (5oz/150g) Steamed Jasmine Rice
 (see page 44)
2 tablespoons chopped lemongrass
1 tablespoon purchased or homemade
 red curry paste
6 green onions, finely chopped
6 kaffir lime leaves, shredded, or 2 teaspoons
 grated lime zest
¹/₄ cup (¹/₄oz/7g) shredded mixed fresh basil and
 coriander leaves
1 egg
1 teaspoon oyster sauce
oil
Chili Lime Sauce (see page 154)

Trim any excess fat from lamb. Cut almost through thicker part of lamb and spread open, overlapping edge with rest of lamb to create a large, flat piece. Combine rice, lemongrass, curry paste, green onions, lime leaves, herbs, egg and oyster sauce in bowl and mix well.

Spoon mixture along center of lamb and roll lamb up firmly, securing with skewers. Tie lamb with kitchen string at ³/₄in (2cm) intervals to keep it firmly rolled. Place lamb on wire rack over roasting pan; brush with oil. Bake in 350°F (180°C) oven about 1 hour or until cooked as desired—test by piercing lamb with skewer in thickest part. (If juices are a little pink, lamb is roasted to medium.) Cover lamb with foil and let stand 10 minutes before slicing. Serve with chili lime sauce.

SERVES 4 TO 6

Thai-Style Ground Beef

Use this mixture to fill pancakes or toasted waffles, or toss through cooked noodles.

10oz (300g) lean ground beef
2 tablespoons chopped lemongrass
1 small onion, finely chopped
2 cloves garlic, crushed
1–2 medium-size red chilies, finely chopped
1 tablespoon oil
2 tablespoons well-flavored beef stock
1 tablespoon oyster sauce
1 tablespoon light soy sauce
2 tablespoons coconut cream
1 teaspoon sugar
¹/₄ cup (¹/₄oz/7g) chopped fresh coriander
lettuce leaves

Combine beef, lemongrass, onion, garlic and chilies in bowl. Cover and refrigerate at least 3 hours to allow flavors to develop.

Heat oil in wok or frying pan. Add beef mixture and stir-fry until all beef has changed color and there are no large lumps. Add stock, sauces, coconut cream and sugar and simmer until thick. Stir in coriander and serve mixture in lettuce leaves.

SERVES 2 TO 4

VARIATIONS

u In place of ground beef, use chopped or sliced boneless sirloin steak. Serve with steamed rice or noodles.

u Drop 6 large Swiss chard leaves in pan of boiling water until just wilted. Drain well. Spoon beef mixture onto leaves, fold in sides of leaves and roll up firmly. Serve with bottled Thai sweet chili sauce.

Slow-Cooked Spicy Beef

Any cut of beef that requires long, slow cooking can be used in this recipe. The slow cooking brings out delicious flavor and makes the meat melt-in-the-mouth tender.

13oz (400g) beef chuck steak
2 tablespoons oil
1–2 tablespoons Penang curry paste
1 small onion, chopped
2 cloves garlic, crushed
1 cup (8fl oz/250ml) well-flavored beef stock
1/4 cup (2fl oz/60ml) coconut cream
2 tablespoons chopped fresh coriander

Remove any excess fat from beef, then cut beef into 1 1/4in (3cm) pieces. Heat oil in medium saucepan, add beef and cook until browned on all sides. Remove from saucepan.

Add curry paste, onion and garlic to saucepan and cook gently until onion is soft. Add beef and stock, cover and simmer, partially covered, 1 hour. Stir in coconut cream and simmer until beef is tender and sauce is thick, about 30 minutes. Stir in coriander and serve immediately.

SERVES 2 TO 4

Lamb with Eggplant and Tamarind

Tamarind concentrate is available from Asian food stores. It is a very thick, almost black liquid made from tamarind pods. It adds a refreshing fruity and tart flavor to dishes such as this.

13oz (400g) boneless lamb
1/4 cup (2fl oz/60ml) oil
1 small onion, finely chopped
1 clove garlic, crushed
1 small eggplant, cubed
1 teaspoon tamarind concentrate
1 tablespoon fish sauce
3/4 cup (6fl oz/185ml) well-flavored
*   chicken stock*
2 tablespoons coconut milk
1–2 medium-size red chilies, chopped
2 tablespoons shredded fresh basil

Trim any fat from lamb and cut lamb into slices 1/2in (1cm) thick. Heat half of oil in wok or large frying pan, add lamb and stir-fry until browned on all sides. Remove from wok.

Heat remaining oil in same wok. Add onion, garlic, eggplant and tamarind concentrate and stir-fry until onion is soft. Stir in fish sauce, stock, coconut milk and chilies and simmer, covered, until the eggplant is soft, about 15 minutes. Add lamb and simmer until just cooked through. Sprinkle with basil and serve immediately.

SERVES 2 TO 4

> ~ *Tip* ~
>
> The safest way to chop chilies is with rubber gloves. Or, if you have only 1 or 2 to chop, hold the chili by the stalk and chop using a pair of kitchen scissors. The hottest part of a chili is its seed, so if you want to reduce the spiciness, remove the seeds.

LEFT: From top: Lamb with Eggplant and Tamarind; Slow-Cooked Spicy Beef

Lamb with Lemongrass and Cashews

I have used both oyster and shiitake mushrooms in this very quick stir-fry. They have wonderfully delicate flavors, so be careful not to overcook them.

10oz (300g) lamb fillets
3 green onions
2½oz (75g) oyster mushrooms
about 1½oz (50g) shiitake mushrooms
1 tablespoon oil
2 cloves garlic, sliced
1 tablespoon chopped lemongrass
1 small green chili, finely chopped
1 small red chili, finely chopped
¼ cup (about 1oz/35g) roasted unsalted cashews
1 tablespoon oyster sauce
2 teaspoons fish sauce
1 tablespoon lime juice
Steamed Rice (see page 49)

Cut lamb into ⅛in (3mm) slices. Cut green onions into 1¼in (3cm) lengths. Cut any large mushrooms in half.

Heat oil in wok or frying pan. Add lamb, garlic and lemongrass and stir-fry 2 minutes. Add green onion, mushrooms, chilies, cashews, oyster sauce, fish sauce and lime juice and stir-fry 1 minute. Serve with steamed rice.

Dry Beef and Sweet Potato Curry

Dry curries are characteristic of Laos. This one is moderately hot, containing 2 small chilies. You may decrease or increase these to suit.

13oz (400g) beef blade steak
1 onion, grated
2 cloves garlic, crushed
1 teaspoon shrimp paste
1 teaspoon ground cumin
2 teaspoons ground coriander
1 tablespoon chopped lemongrass
½ teaspoon galangal powder
½ teaspoon ground turmeric
1 teaspoon paprika
1 teaspoon grated lime zest
1 tablespoon oil
¾ cup (6fl oz/185ml) water
10oz (300g) sweet potato, chopped
1 small red chili, finely chopped
1 small green chili, finely chopped
1 teaspoon cumin seeds

Cut beef into 1¼in (3cm) pieces. Using mortar and pestle or blender, grind onion, garlic, shrimp paste, cumin, coriander, lemongrass, galangal, turmeric, paprika and lime zest to paste consistency.

Heat oil in wok or frying pan. Add beef and stir-fry until browned. Drain on paper towels.

Add paste mixture to wok and stir-fry about 1 minute or until aromatic. Return beef to wok with water and simmer, covered, 30 minutes. Add sweet potato and simmer uncovered 10 more minutes or until sweet potato and beef are tender. Sprinkle curry with chilies and cumin seeds before serving.

SERVES 2

Aromatic Beef Casserole with Fennel and Daikon

During the long, slow cooking process, the beef becomes beautifully tender and absorbs the flavors of the fennel and daikon radish. Serve this casserole with crusty French bread or a bowl of steamed rice.

1lb (450g) beef chuck steak
1 tablespoon finely chopped lemongrass
1 red chili, finely chopped
1 tablespoon grated fresh ginger
1 teaspoon cinnamon
1 teaspoon curry powder
1 tablespoon fish sauce
1 tablespoon oil
1 small onion, finely chopped
3 cloves garlic, crushed
1 tablespoon tomato paste
1 cup (8fl oz/250ml) water
1 cup (8fl oz/250ml) well-flavored beef stock
½ small fennel bulb, sliced
1 small carrot, chopped
3½oz (100g) daikon radish, chopped
1 medium potato, chopped

Trim excess fat from beef. Cut beef into 2in (5cm) pieces.

Combine lemongrass, chili, ginger, cinnamon and curry powder and fish sauce in bowl. Add beef and stir until well coated. Cover and refrigerate 1 hour.

Heat oil in wok or frying pan. Add beef in 2 batches and stir-fry until well browned. Drain on paper towels. Add onion and garlic to wok and stir-fry about 1 minute or until aromatic. Return beef to wok with tomato paste, water and beef stock and simmer, covered, 1 hour.

Add fennel, carrot, daikon and potato, cover and simmer 30 minutes or until beef and vegetables are tender.

SERVES 2 TO 4

Beef in Coconut Milk with Baby Onions

Another quick and easy stir-fry. It is important to have all ingredients ready before you start cooking. Use lamb or pork fillet instead of the beef, if you like, and serve with some chili sauce on the table for diners to add as they like.

12oz (350g) beef round steak
1 small green or red bell pepper
1 tablespoon oil
1 teaspoon curry powder
1 teaspoon galangal powder
½ teaspoon dried chili flakes
2 small brown pickling onions, sliced into rings
¼ cup (2fl oz/60ml) coconut cream
2 teaspoons light soy sauce
1 tablespoon shredded coconut, toasted

Trim any excess fat from beef. Cut across grain into ⅛in (3mm) strips. Cut bell pepper into thin strips.

Heat oil in wok or frying pan. Add beef, curry powder, galangal and chili flakes and stir-fry 2 minutes. Add bell pepper and onions, and stir-fry 1 minute. Add coconut cream and soy sauce and stir-fry until well combined and heated through. Serve sprinkled with coconut.

SERVES 2

VARIATION

More vegetables can be added to this dish if you like. Choose from broccoli florets, cauliflower florets, button mushrooms, fresh asparagus pieces or chopped daikon radish. Add a total of about 7oz (200g) prepared vegetables

Grilled Lamb and Eggplant with Ginger Sauce

A wonderfully easy dish to prepare, this can be made several hours ahead and eaten cold.

6 lamb scallops
3 cloves garlic, crushed
¼ teaspoon freshly ground black pepper
2 long baby eggplants
oil
1 tablespoon chopped fresh coriander
GINGER SAUCE
Fish Dipping Sauce (see page 155)
1 teaspoon grated fresh ginger
1 tablespoon bean sauce

Combine lamb with garlic and pepper in medium bowl, cover and refrigerate 1 hour. Halve eggplants lengthwise.

Barbecue or grill lamb and eggplants on well oiled grid until browned and just cooked.

For ginger sauce, combine the fish dipping sauce and ginger and bean sauce in small pitcher or bowl.

Arrange lamb and eggplant on serving plate. Drizzle with ginger sauce and garnish with coriander.

SERVES 2

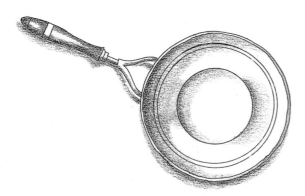

Beefsteaks with Slivered Mango and Vegetables

This recipe makes quite a hearty quantity of vegetables. The sauce is excellent over barbecued meat. Substitute beef round or fillet if you prefer.

3 tablespoons oil
2 New York cut beef steaks
1 small red bell pepper
1 small green bell pepper
1 small carrot
2 spring (bulb) onions
2 tablespoons light soy sauce
1 tablespoon rice vinegar
1 tablespoon fish sauce
1 teaspoon cornstarch
¼ cup (2fl oz/60ml) water
¼ teaspoon hot chili sauce
¼ cup (¼oz/7g) fresh mint leaves
1 medium mango, sliced
fresh coriander sprigs

Heat 2 tablespoons oil in frying pan and cook steaks until well browned on both sides and cooked to desired doneness. Drain on paper towels and keep warm.

While steaks are cooking, prepare vegetables. Cut peppers and carrot into long, thin strips. Quarter spring onions lengthwise, including some of green tops.

Heat remaining 1 tablespoon oil in same pan. Add peppers, carrot and spring onions and stir-fry until lightly browned, about 3 minutes. Add soy sauce, vinegar and fish sauce. Blend cornstarch with water and chili sauce, add to pan and bring to boil. Add mint and mango, remove from heat and stir well.

Cut steaks into thin strips or leave whole. Serve mango and vegetable mixture with steaks. Drizzle steaks with pan juices and garnish with coriander.

SERVES 2

RIGHT: From top: Grilled Lamb and Eggplant with Ginger Sauce; Beefsteaks with Slivered Mango and Vegetables

The Herbs and Spices of Indochina

Ground Cumin

Ground Turmeric

Galangal Powder

Five Spice Powder

Paprika

Black Pepper

Mint

Dried Galangal

Ground Coriander

Beef in Peanut Sauce

Penang curry paste is available from Asian food stores. You will usually find it in a small can. I use what I need from the can and spoon the rest into a clean jar to keep in the refrigerator for up to 2 months (it is usually used by then).

1½ tablespoons Penang curry paste
4 kaffir lime leaves or 1–2 teaspoons grated lime zest
½ cup (4fl oz/125ml) well-flavored beef or chicken stock
¾ cup (6fl oz/185ml) coconut milk
13oz (400g) beef round steak or boneless sirloin steak, thinly sliced
1 tablespoon fish sauce
⅓ cup (1½oz/50g) ground roasted peanuts
1 medium-size red chili, sliced
½ cup (½oz/15g) mixed fresh basil and coriander leaves
1 green onion, chopped

Combine curry paste, lime leaves, stock and coconut milk in saucepan. Bring to boil; boil 1 minute. Add beef, fish sauce, peanuts and chili. Simmer until beef is just cooked, about 10 minutes. Stir in herbs and green onion and serve immediately.

SERVES 2 TO 4

VARIATIONS
◆ Substitute lamb or chicken for beef.
◆ Add a handful of green peas to sauce with beef.

Lamb's Liver with Garlic and Black Pepper

This dish can also be made with chicken livers or calf's liver. Make sure you remove the thin membrane from around the liver, as it can be a little chewy. Don't overcook the liver.

13oz (400g) lamb's liver
2 tablespoons lemon juice
2 tablespoons oil
4 cloves garlic, finely chopped
4 coriander roots, finely chopped
1 teaspoon coarsely ground black peppercorns
1 tablespoon fish sauce
2 tablespoons chopped fresh coriander leaves
1 tablespoon lime juice

Soak liver in bowl of cold water with lemon juice 30 minutes. Drain. Peel away thin membrane from outside of liver.

Cut liver into slices about ½in (1.5cm) thick. Heat oil in large frying pan, add liver and cook over high heat until slices are browned on both sides and just cooked through. Remove from pan.

Add garlic, coriander roots and peppercorns to pan and cook gently for a few seconds. Stir in fish sauce, coriander leaves and lime juice. Add liver and simmer until heated through. Serve immediately.

SERVES 2 TO 4

LEFT: Lamb's Liver with Garlic and Black Pepper

Salads and Vegetables

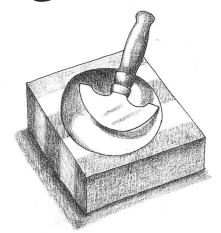

Raw salads and vegetable dishes form the basis of any Vietnamese, Laotian or Cambodian meal. Pickled vegetables can be decoratively cut and arranged to accompany a rice or seafood dish.

The flavors and ingredients of Thailand add great interest and a myriad of textures to vegetables and salads. Some of the salads make perfect luncheon dishes that are light and nutritious; the vegetable dishes work well with soups and curries. The ingredients are readily available, and you will find these dishes simple to prepare.

RIGHT: Spicy Eggplant and Shredded Chicken

Greens with Chili and Herbs

This dish can be made with any of the leafy green vegetables. I have used chicory, which is very nutritious and combines well with Vietnamese flavorings.

1lb (450g) chicory
2 tablespoons oil
4 cloves garlic, finely chopped
2 small red chilies, finely chopped
2 tablespoons shredded fresh mint
1 tablespoon fresh coriander leaves
1½ tablespoons vegetable stock
1 tablespoon fish sauce

Trim stalks from chicory. Wash stalks and leaves thoroughly; drain well. Cut stalks into finger-length pieces.

Half fill large saucepan with water and bring to boil. Add chicory stalks and boil 1 minute. Add leaves and boil gently until stalks and leaves are tender, about 3 more minutes. Drain.

Heat oil in saucepan, add garlic and chilies and cook until aromatic. Then add herbs, stock and fish sauce and simmer 1 minute.

Return chicory to pan and toss well until heated through.

SERVES 2 TO 4

Spicy Eggplant with Shredded Chicken

The flavors of barbecued eggplant, pepper and chicken with lots of fresh herbs make this dish delicious. Only a minimal amount of oil is used. This is even better if made up to 3 hours ahead, because the flavors have time to develop.

2 long baby eggplants
1 single chicken breast fillet
1 small long green banana pepper, quartered
1 small tomato, sliced
2 cloves garlic, sliced
2 teaspoons chopped fresh mint
1 tablespoon chopped fresh coriander
1 small red chili, finely chopped
DRESSING
2 tablespoons fish sauce
1½ tablespoons rice vinegar
½ teaspoon sesame oil

Cut eggplants lengthwise into slices ¼in (5mm) thick. Barbecue or broil chicken until cooked. Cool slightly, then cut into thin shreds.

Barbecue or broil eggplants and pepper until lightly browned; pepper skin will bubble and burn. Place pepper in paper or plastic bag until cool enough to handle. Remove skin and seeds and slice pepper into thin strips.

Combine chicken, eggplant, pepper, tomato, garlic, mint, coriander and chili in bowl.

For dressing, combine fish sauce, vinegar and sesame oil in jar and shake well. Pour dressing over chicken and vegetables. Serve warm or refrigerate for 1 hour before serving.

SERVES 2

Pickled Vegetables with Bacon

If you haven't the time to make the pickled carrot and cucumber, you will find a variety of pickled vegetables at any Asian grocery store that will work just as well in this recipe; you will need about 12 oz (350g) of vegetables. If you can't find fresh mini corn, use half a can.

1 tablespoon oil
3 cloves garlic, sliced
1¼in (3cm) piece fresh ginger, peeled and
   thinly sliced
3 slices bacon, chopped
2½oz (75g) fresh mini corn, halved lengthwise
2½oz (75g) snow peas
3 green onions, sliced
Pickled Carrot (see recipe at right), drained
Pickled Cucumber (see recipe at right), drained
1 can (7oz/230g) sliced bamboo shoots, drained
1 tablespoon rice vinegar
1 tablespoon fish sauce
1 tablespoon bean sauce
2 teaspoons lime juice

Heat oil in wok or frying pan. Add garlic, ginger and bacon and stir-fry 2 minutes. Add corn and stir-fry 3 minutes. Add snow peas, green onion, pickled carrot and pickled cucumber and stir-fry 2 minutes.

Add bamboo shoots, vinegar, fish sauce, bean sauce and lime juice and stir until heated through.

SERVES 2

VARIATION
In place of bacon use Chinese barbecued pork.

Pickled Carrot, Daikon Radish or Cucumber

This is a very easy way of pickling vegetables. Because they are not actually boiled, they are nice and crisp, with plenty of flavor. A classic accompaniment for many Vietnamese meals, these can be made ahead and are perfect with cocktails or on a buffet table.

2 small carrots, 5oz (150g) daikon radish or
   2 small cucumbers
½ cup (4fl oz/125ml) rice vinegar
2 teaspoons sugar
¼ teaspoon salt
½ cup (4fl oz/125ml) boiling water

Peel carrots or daikon, cut into slices ⅛in (3mm) thick. If using cucumbers, cut into slices as for carrots but do not peel.

Combine vinegar, sugar, salt and boiling water in bowl and stir until sugar and salt have dissolved. Cool to room temperature. Add vegetables and let stand at least 2 hours before using.

Store in jar in refrigerator, being sure that vegetables are fully covered by vinegar mixture to prevent any mold from forming. Pickled vegetables will keep refrigerated up to 2 weeks.

MAKES ABOUT 1 MEDIUM JAR

Lamb Patty Salad

The lamb patties can be added warm or cold. This makes a lovely summer
main course salad.

13oz (400g) lean ground lamb
1 tablespoon grated fresh ginger
1 teaspoon grated lime zest
2 cloves garlic, crushed
6 green onions, finely chopped
1 egg
1 teaspoon sambal oelek
1 tablespoon oil
1 bunch arugula
3¹/₂oz (100g) snow peas
1 small red bell pepper, thinly sliced
DRESSING
2 tablespoons oil
1 tablespoon lime juice
1 clove garlic, crushed
salt and black pepper

Shape tablespoons of mixture into patties. Heat oil
in large frying pan. Add lamb patties and cook until
browned on both sides and just cooked through. Drain
on paper towels.

Tear arugula into large pieces. Drop snow peas into
saucepan of boiling water and boil 1 minute. Drain
snow peas, rinse under cold water and drain
thoroughly. For dressing, combine all ingredients in
screw-top jar and shake well.

Arrange lamb patties, arugula, snow peas and bell
pepper on serving plates; drizzle with dressing.

SERVES 4 AS AN ENTREE

OR

2 AS A MAIN COURSE

Combine lamb, ginger, lime zest, garlic, green onion,
egg and sambal oelek in bowl and mix thoroughly.

Shape tablespoons of mixture into patties.

Drain cooked patties on paper towels.

RIGHT: Lamb Patty Salad

Glazed Pumpkin and Zucchini

Another easy yet flavorful way with vegetables, this is best served with meat or seafood dishes such as Lemongrass and Chili Chicken (page 70), Broiled Crab and Shrimp Cakes (page 106), or Dry Beef and Sweet Potato Curry (page 120). I have chosen to leave the skin on the pumpkin as it looks more attractive, and the skin is edible if the pumpkin is very young.

12oz (350g) small pumpkin
2 medium zucchini
1 tablespoon oil
2 cloves garlic, halved
1¼in (3cm) piece fresh ginger, peeled and finely shredded
2 teaspoons fish sauce
1 tablespoon honey
¼ cup (2fl oz/60ml) well-flavored vegetable or chicken stock
2 teaspoons sesame seeds, toasted

Cut unpeeled pumpkin into wedges about ¾in (2cm) thick. Halve zucchini lengthwise and cut each half into thirds.

Heat oil in wok or large frying pan. Add zucchini and cook over high heat until browned on all sides. Drain on paper towels. Add pumpkin and brown on both sides, then add garlic and ginger and stir-fry about 1 minute or until aromatic.

Add fish sauce, honey and stock and bring to boil. Cover and simmer 3 minutes. Return zucchini to pan and simmer, covered, until vegetables are tender, about 2 more minutes. Serve sprinkled with sesame seeds.

SERVES 2

Grapefruit, Sprout and Cucumber Salad

A beautifully crisp, light and healthy salad that is a delicious meal in itself or a perfect accompaniment for a banquet meal. I've used the delicately flavored pink grapefruit for its pretty color, but it is not always readily available, so yellow grapefruit can be used.

1 small pink or yellow grapefruit
1 small cucumber
5oz (150g) cooked chicken, shredded
4 cooked medium shrimp, peeled, deveined and halved
1 small carrot, grated
1 cup (2½oz/80g) bean sprouts
1 cup (2½oz/80g) snow pea sprouts
1 tablespoon fresh mint leaves
1 tablespoon fresh coriander leaves
1 tablespoon unsalted roasted cashews
Fish Dipping Sauce (see page 155)

Peel and segment grapefruit. Halve cucumber lengthwise; using teaspoon, scoop out seeds. Slice cucumber.

Combine grapefruit, cucumber, chicken, shrimp, carrot, sprouts and herbs in bowl. Sprinkle with cashews, cover and refrigerate up to 2 hours. Before serving, drizzle with fish dipping sauce.

SERVES 2 TO 4

VARIATION

Substitute any cooked meat for chicken and shrimp or broil a single chicken breast fillet until just cooked, then cool, slice and add to salad.

RIGHT: From top: Glazed Pumpkin and Zucchini; Grapefruit, Sprout and Cucumber Salad

Vegetable Salad with Chili Lime Dressing

This salad can be made a day ahead. Combine with the dressing before serving.

1 carrot
3¹/₂oz (100) green beans
5oz (150g) broccoli
1 red bell pepper
6 green onions, chopped
2 tablespoons chopped fresh mint
2 tablespoons chopped fresh coriander
CHILI LIME DRESSING
¹/₂ teaspoon grated lime zest
1¹/₂ tablespoons lime juice
1 teaspoon light soy sauce
1 tablespoon sweet chili sauce
1 tablespoon oil

Cut carrot into thin sticks. Cut beans into 2in (5cm) lengths. Cut broccoli into small florets. Cut bell pepper into 2in (5cm) strips. Cook carrot, beans and broccoli separately in saucepan of boiling water until almost tender. Drain, rinse under cold water and drain well.

For chili lime dressing, combine all ingredients in a screw-top jar and shake well.

Combine cooked vegetables with bell pepper, green onion, mint, coriander and dressing in serving bowl and toss well.

SERVES 4

Chicken, Scallop and Orange Salad

Shrimp can be used in place of the scallops in this fresh-flavored salad. If you are preparing it ahead, peel the avocado and add to the salad at the last minute.

2 single chicken breast fillets
3¹/₂oz (100g) scallops
6 green onion tops, sliced
1 orange, segmented
3¹/₂oz (100g) canned bamboo shoot, julienned
1 avocado, sliced
DRESSING
2 tablespoons oil
2 tablespoons orange juice
1 teaspoon grated lime zest
2 tablespoons chopped fresh coriander
1 teaspoon fish sauce

Place chicken in small frying pan and cover with water or chicken stock. Cover and simmer until just cooked through, about 10 minutes. Remove from pan and cool. Add scallops to liquid in frying pan and simmer until just opaque, about 2 minutes. Drain scallops and cool.

For dressing, combine all ingredients in screw-top jar and shake well. Slice chicken. Combine chicken, scallops, green onion tops, orange segments, bamboo shoot and avocado in bowl. Add dressing and toss gently. Serve immediately.

SERVES 2 TO 4

VARIATION

Use half a purchased barbecued chicken and cooked shrimp in place of chicken fillets and scallops. Slice chicken meat, discarding skin and fat. Peel and devein shrimp.

Thai Beef Salad

This traditional Thai salad is refreshingly spicy. You can make the beef mixture a day ahead if you like—this allows the flavors to develop.

12oz (375g) piece boneless sirloin steak
4 green onions, sliced
1 tablespoon shredded fresh mint
1 tablespoon fresh coriander leaves
2 tablespoons lime juice
1 tablespoon oil
2 teaspoons fish sauce
1 teaspoon light soy sauce
1 clove garlic, crushed
1 small red chili, finely chopped
Boston or butter lettuce leaves

Trim any fat from steak. Broil or panfry steak until medium rare; remove and cool.

Cut steak into thin strips. Combine with green onion, mint, coriander, lime juice, oil, fish sauce, soy sauce, garlic and chili in bowl. Spoon mixture onto lettuce and serve immediately.

SERVES 2 TO 4

VARIATION

Lamb leg steaks or butterflied pork steaks can be used in place of the beef.

Fish Salad with Mint and Beans

Choose a firm fish fillet that will hold together when cooked. If you cannot find snake beans (yardlong beans), substitute green beans.

1 tablespoon oil
7oz (200g) boneless white fish fillet, thinly sliced
3$\frac{1}{2}$oz (100g) snake beans (yardlong beans), cut into 1in (2.5cm) lengths
2$\frac{1}{2}$oz (80g) small snow peas
$\frac{1}{2}$ small green oakleaf lettuce, torn
$\frac{1}{2}$ cup ($\frac{1}{2}$oz/15g) small fresh mint leaves
DRESSING
2 tablespoons oil
2 green onions, finely chopped
2 tablespoons lime juice
2 teaspoons fish sauce
$\frac{1}{2}$ teaspoon sugar
$\frac{1}{4}$ teaspoon chili powder

Heat oil in wok or large frying pan. Add fish a handful at a time and cook, turning gently and without breaking, until cooked through. Remove from wok and let cool.

Drop beans and snow peas into saucepan of boiling water and boil about 1 minute. Drain, rinse well under cold water and drain thoroughly.

For dressing, combine all ingredients in screw-top jar and shake well.

Combine beans, snow peas, lettuce leaves, mint and dressing in serving bowl. Add fish and toss gently to combine.

SERVES 2 TO 4

Tomato, Pepper and Chili Relish

This relish is delicious served with grilled or barbecued meats, poultry or fish. It will keep for several days in the refrigerator.

7oz (200g) cherry tomatoes
1 small red bell pepper, quartered
1 small green bell pepper, quartered
2–4 red chilies
6 green onions, finely chopped
1 tablespoon oil
1 tablespoon lime juice
2 teaspoons fish sauce
1/2 teaspoon sugar
1 tablespoon chopped fresh coriander
1 clove garlic, crushed

Place tomatoes in shallow broiler pan. Add pepper, skin side up, and chilies. Broil until pepper skins are blackened and blistered, removing any cherry tomatoes or chilies that are becoming too browned. Cool all vegetables.

Remove skin from peppers. Chop peppers, tomatoes and chilies very finely. Combine with green onion, oil, lime juice, fish sauce, sugar, coriander and garlic in bowl and mix thoroughly.

SERVES 4

Carrot, Kohlrabi and Zucchini Salad

This simple but terrific salad is very easy to prepare, especially if you have a food processor with a grater attachment.

1 tablespoon dried shrimp, finely chopped
2 cloves garlic, finely chopped
1 medium-size red chili, finely chopped
1/2 teaspoon tamarind concentrate
1 teaspoon sugar
2 teaspoons fish sauce
1/4 cup (about 1oz/35g) ground roasted peanuts
1 tablespoon lime juice
2 tablespoons oil
1 large carrot, grated
1 large zucchini, grated
2 purple or green kohlrabi, peeled and grated

Combine dried shrimp, garlic, chili, tamarind concentrate, sugar, fish sauce, peanuts, lime juice and oil in bowl.

Add carrot, zucchini and kohlrabi to peanut mixture. Mix very well to combine flavors. Let stand 2 hours before serving.

SERVES 4

VARIATION
Substitute green papaya, butternut squash, green mango or turnip for kohlrabi.

RIGHT: Tomato, Pepper and Chili Relish

Eggplant Salad

This salad makes an excellent accompaniment for a barbecue. If long baby eggplants are not available, use small regular eggplants and cut them into smaller pieces once they are cooked.

8 long baby eggplants
oil
2 teaspoons fish sauce
2 teaspoons light soy sauce
^{1}/$_2$ teaspoon sesame oil
1 clove garlic, crushed
^{1}/$_2$ teaspoon brown sugar
2 green onions, finely chopped
1 tablespoon chopped fresh basil or mint
^{1}/$_2$–1 teaspoon sambal oelek

Cut eggplants diagonally into slices ^{1}/$_2$in (1cm) thick. Brush with oil and broil or grill until browned and soft. Let cool.

Toss eggplant with fish sauce, soy sauce, sesame oil, garlic, brown sugar, green onion, basil and sambal oelek in bowl and mix thoroughly. Let stand 1 hour before serving.

SERVES 4

Vegetable Stir-Fry

Any Chinese greens can be used in this stir-fry.

1 tablespoon oil
2 cloves garlic, crushed
12 spears fresh asparagus, quartered
1 red bell pepper, thinly sliced
4oz (125g) broccoli, cut into small florets
1 bunch choy sum or other Chinese greens, shredded
6 green onions, chopped
1 tablespoon fish sauce
1 tablespoon sambal oelek
4 kaffir lime leaves, shredded, or 1–2 teaspoons grated lime zest

Heat oil in wok or large frying pan. Add garlic, asparagus, bell pepper and broccoli and stir-fry until almost tender. Add choy sum, green onion, fish sauce, sambal oelek and lime leaves and stir-fry until choy sum is wilted and vegetables are crisp-tender.

SERVES 2 TO 4

Greens and Reds in Spicy Sauce

Bok choy is available from Asian food stores and produce markets.

10 fresh asparagus spears, cut into 1in (2.5cm) lengths
3^1/$_2$oz (100g) green beans, cut into 1in (2.5cm) lengths
1 small head radicchio
1 small bunch short-stemmed bok choy or other Chinese greens
2 tablespoons oil
2 cloves garlic, crushed
2 tablespoons chopped lemongrass
2 teaspoons grated fresh ginger
1 teaspoon ground cumin
1 tablespoon fish sauce
1 tablespoon sweet chili sauce
2 tablespoons chopped fresh coriander

Drop asparagus and beans into saucepan of boiling water and boil until just tender, about 1 minute. Drain well. Tear radicchio leaves in half. Cut stalks from bok choy, then cut leaves in half.

Heat oil in wok or large frying pan. Add garlic, lemongrass, ginger and cumin and cook gently several seconds. Add asparagus, beans and bok choy stalks and stir-fry for 1 minute. Add bok choy leaves and radicchio with all remaining ingredients and stir-fry until leaves are barely wilted. Serve immediately.

SERVES 2 TO 4

Barbecued Duck Salad

You can buy barbecued duck from Chinese delis. They are usually quite happy to sell a half duck. If you prefer, you can use a barbecued chicken.

1/2 Chinese barbecued duck
8 large romaine lettuce leaves, coarsely shredded
1/4 cup (1/4oz/7g) fresh coriander leaves
DRESSING
2 tablespoons oil
2 tablespoons lime juice
1/4 teaspoon sesame oil
2 teaspoons fish sauce
1/4 teaspoon chili powder
4 green onions, finely chopped
1/2 teaspoon sugar

Remove all meat and skin from duck bones. Remove skin and all fat from meat. Slice duck meat thinly. Slice any lean crisp skin thinly and discard fatty skin. Combine duck meat and skin with lettuce and coriander in bowl.

For dressing, combine all ingredients in screw-top jar and shake well. Pour dressing over duck mixture and toss well before serving.

SERVES 2 TO 4

VARIATION
Fresh spinach or Boston lettuce can be used in place of romaine.

Noodle and Bean Salad

Broad beans are much more attractive with their outer skins removed, but if you are pressed for time, ignore this step. Serving this salad is made simpler if you cut the noodles into 2in (5cm) lengths.

3 1/2oz (100g) frozen or fresh shelled broad beans
6 1/2oz (200g) green beans, cut into 1in (2.5cm) lengths
6oz (180g) thin fresh egg noodles, cut into shorter lengths
DRESSING
1/4 cup (2fl oz/60ml) oil
2 tablespoons lime juice
1 clove garlic, crushed
1 teaspoon fish sauce
2 green onions, finely chopped
2 tablespoons chopped fresh coriander

Drop broad beans into large saucepan of boiling water; boil until tender, about 5 minutes. Remove beans using slotted spoon and rinse under cold water. Drain well.

Add green beans and noodles to same saucepan of water and boil 2 minutes. Drain, rinse under cold water and drain thoroughly.

For dressing, combine all ingredients in jar with a screw-top lid and shake well. Remove outer skins from broad beans. Combine all beans, noodles and dressing in bowl and toss well to combine.

SERVES 2 TO 4

Green Papaya, Pork and Carrot Salad

Green papaya may be available at your local produce market or at an Asian food store that sells fresh fruit and vegetables. If it is unavailable, substitute green mango or turnip. The pork can be cooked a day ahead.

1 tablespoon dried shrimp
3½oz (100g) pork fillet
1 tablespoon finely chopped lemongrass
1 small fresh chili, seeded and finely chopped
1 teaspoon honey
½ teaspoon fish sauce
1 teaspoon light soy sauce
½ small (about 2½oz/75g) green unripe papaya
1 small carrot
1 small cucumber
1 tablespoon shredded fresh mint leaves
1 tablespoon shredded fresh coriander leaves
DRESSING
Fish Dipping Sauce (see page 155)
1–2 teaspoons hot chili sauce

Cover shrimp with hot water in bowl and let stand 30 minutes. Drain, then chop finely. Cut pork into slices ⅛in (3mm) thick.

Using mortar and pestle or blender, grind lemongrass, chili, honey, fish sauce and soy sauce to paste consistency. Combine pork with chili mixture in small bowl and mix well. Cover and refrigerate at least 1 hour or overnight.

Arrange pork slices in single layer on wire rack in a roasting pan and bake in 350°F (180°C) oven until just cooked, about 20 minutes. Let cool. Cut into thin strips.

Using sharp knife, cut papaya, carrot and cucumber into long, very thin strips; they will stay crispier this way; otherwise, coarsely grate lengthwise.

Combine shrimp, pork, papaya, carrot, cucumber, mint and coriander in serving bowl.

For dressing, combine fish dipping sauce and chili sauce in jar with screw-top lid and shake well. Pour dressing over salad and serve.

SERVES 2 TO 4

Arrange pork slices on wire rack in roasting pan.

Cut papaya, carrot and cucumber into thin strips.

RIGHT: Green Papaya, Pork and Carrot Salad

Vegetable Platter with Dipping Sauce

A vegetable platter is a must for any Vietnamese banquet, especially with such dishes as Oven-Baked Marinated Pork Fillet (page 30) or Steamed Whole Fish with Lemongrass and Chili (page 102). Use any variety of lettuces, vegetables or sprouts that are in season.

1 small cucumber
½ bunch fresh asparagus spears, trimmed
½ cup (about ½oz/20g) alfalfa and onion sprouts
1 small tomato, cut into 8 wedges
¼ cup (¼oz/7g) fresh mint leaves
¼ cup (¼oz/7g) fresh coriander leaves
1 carambola (star fruit), sliced
assorted lettuce leaves such as red oakleaf,
*   radicchio and romaine*
Fish Dipping Sauce or Peanut Sauce
*   (see page 155)*

Slice cucumber lengthwise into thin strips. Drop asparagus into saucepan of boiling water and boil until just tender. Drain and rinse under cold water; drain well.

Arrange cucumber, asparagus, sprouts, tomato, herbs, carambola (star fruit) and lettuces leaves on serving platter. Each person should take a lettuce leaf, fill it with some vegetables and herbs and perhaps some meat, such as the marinated pork fillet, form a bundle and dip it in sauce before eating.

SERVES 2 TO 4 PEOPLE

Chicken and Basil Salad

This lovely salad is perfect for a summer lunch. It can be prepared ahead to be served cold. Just keep the cooked chicken mixture separate until you are ready to serve.

2 celery stalks
1 small carrot
2 green onions
6 leaves red oakleaf lettuce
1 small red onion, thinly sliced
1 tablespoon oil
3 cloves garlic, sliced
1 single chicken breast fillet, thinly sliced
2 tablespoons fresh basil leaves
2 tablespoons fresh mint leaves
2 tablespoons fish sauce
⅓ cup (2½fl oz/80ml) lime juice
1 tablespoon rice vinegar
2 teaspoons sweet chili sauce

Cut celery, carrot and green onion into thin strips about 2½in (6cm) long.

Arrange lettuce leaves on serving plates. Combine celery, carrot, green onion and onion in bowl and pile into lettuce leaves.

Heat oil in frying pan, add garlic and stir about 1 minute or until aromatic. Add chicken and stir-fry 2 minutes, then add herbs and stir-fry until they have wilted and chicken is cooked. Remove from heat and add fish sauce, lime juice, vinegar and sweet chili sauce, stirring until well combined. Spoon chicken mixture over vegetables and drizzle with pan juices.

SERVES 2

VARIATION
Use 7oz (200g) pork or beef in place of chicken.

Green Beans with Cauliflower and Scallops

If possible, buy scallops with the orange roe (coral) attached. Their creamy white and orange colors look beautiful with the vegetables.

3½oz (100g) scallops, preferably with roe attached
2 teaspoons fish sauce
2 cloves garlic, crushed
¼ teaspoon freshly ground black pepper
1 onion
3½oz (100g) green beans
8oz (250g) cauliflower
1 tablespoon oil
1 tablespoon chopped lemongrass
1 tablespoon grated fresh ginger
2 teaspoons light soy sauce
½ cup (4fl oz/125ml) fish stock or water
1 tablespoon lime juice

Combine scallops, fish sauce, garlic and pepper in a small bowl, cover and refrigerate 1 hour.

Cut onion into thin wedges. Cut beans into 2in (5cm) lengths. Cut cauliflower into florets.

Heat oil in wok or frying pan. Add onion, lemongrass and ginger and stir-fry 1 minute. Add cauliflower, soy sauce and stock. Bring to boil, reduce heat and simmer, covered, 3 minutes. Add scallop mixture and beans and simmer, covered, for 2 more minutes or until scallops are just cooked. Stir in lime juice and serve.

SERVES 2

VARIATION
Fresh uncooked shrimp may be substituted for the scallops.

Lamb, Lime and Watercress Salad

Prepare the salad up to 2 hours ahead and drizzle with dressing just before serving.

7oz (200g) lamb fillet
2 cloves garlic, crushed
1 tablespoon lime juice
2 teaspoons peanut butter
pinch chili powder
2 teaspoons oil
3 cups (5oz/150g) fresh watercress
1 small red onion, sliced into rings
1oz (30g) sugar snap peas, halved
1 small red bell pepper, finely chopped
2 teaspoons finely chopped roasted peanuts
DRESSING
1 tablespoon sweet chili sauce
2 teaspoons fish sauce
¼ cup (2fl oz/60ml) lime juice
1 tablespoon oil
2 teaspoons grated fresh ginger
1 tablespoon water

Cut lamb into thin strips. Combine lamb, garlic, lime juice, peanut butter and chili powder in small bowl, cover and refrigerate 1 hour.

Heat oil in wok or frying pan until very hot. Add lamb and stir-fry quickly until just cooked; drain on paper towels and cool.

For dressing, combine all dressing ingredients in jar with a screw-top lid and shake well.

Combine watercress, onion, sugar snap peas, bell pepper and lamb in large bowl. Drizzle with dressing and sprinkle with peanuts.

SERVES 2 TO 4

VARIATION
Beef fillet or chicken breast fillet may be substituted for lamb.

Desserts

Thais are fond of their desserts, but they are usually reserved for more formal dinners. An everyday meal does not normally include a dessert, but dessert-type snacks are often purchased from street vendors during the day—deep-fried bananas being a favorite along with sticky rice sweets.

The Vietnamese, Laotians and Cambodians do not have desserts often, although they do eat lovely baked sweets and pastries that reveal a strong French influence.

The desserts in this section can be served with coffee, as part of an Asian meal or to conclude a dinner party. They are mostly simple and, as with many Asian desserts, use fruit and coconut as the basic ingredients.

RIGHT: Coconut Ice Cream and
Mango with Lime and Ginger

Yam Coconut Puddings

These puddings are very simple to make and can be eaten hot or at room temperature. It is best not to boil the yam as it can become a little too wet—steaming produces a better texture.

9oz (275g) yam, peeled and chopped
1 cup (8fl oz/250ml) coconut milk
1/3 cup (2oz/60g) brown sugar
2 eggs
flaked almonds
mango slices or strawberries

Steam or microwave yam until cooked. Let cool. Combine yam, coconut milk, sugar and eggs in blender and puree until smooth.

Pour mixture into four 1/2 cup (4fl oz/125ml) ramekins. Sprinkle tops with almonds. Bake in 350°F (180°C) oven until centers of puddings are set, about 20 minutes. Serve with a slice of mango or with strawberries.

SERVES 4

VARIATIONS
◆ Add 3 tablespoons golden raisins.
◆ Add 1 teaspoon grated fresh ginger and 2 tablespoons finely chopped candied ginger.
◆ Add 1 teaspoon each grated lime zest and grated orange zest.

Coconut Ice Cream and Mango with Lime and Ginger

You can either scoop this ice cream or turn it out of the pan and cut it into thick slices. It is usually best to make the ice cream a day ahead. It can also be made in an ice cream machine.

1 cup (8fl oz/250ml) coconut milk
3/4 cup (6fl oz/185ml) whipping cream
1/4 cup (2 1/2oz/75g) sugar
2 tablespoons coconut, toasted
2 eggs
1 mango, peeled and sliced
1in (2.5cm) piece fresh ginger, julienned
1 tablespoon sugar
1 teaspoon grated lime zest
2 tablespoons lime juice

Combine coconut milk, cream, 1/4 cup sugar and coconut in saucepan and bring to boil. Whisk eggs in heatproof bowl, until combined. Whisk boiling coconut milk mixture into eggs. Let cool.

Pour mixture into small loaf pan, cover and freeze until firm. Chop ice cream, then beat in bowl with electric mixer or in food processor until smooth. Spoon mixture back into pan (line pan with foil if you wish to turn out ice cream for serving). Cover and freeze several hours until firm. (Alternatively, prepare ice cream in ice cream maker according to manufacturer's instructions.)

Combine mango, ginger, 1 tablespoon sugar, lime zest and juice in bowl. Cover and refrigerate several hours to allow flavors to combine. Serve ice cream in slices or scoops with mango mixture.

SERVES 4

Crisp Bananas with Caramel Sauce

I don't usually like to deep-fry foods, but this is an exception. The bananas are lovely and crisp on the outside and go beautifully with the rich caramel sauce.

3 bananas
2 tablespoons grated palm sugar or brown sugar
2 tablespoons coconut, toasted
$^1/_2$ cup ($2^1/_2$oz/75g) rice flour
1 tablespoon sesame seeds
2 tablespoons sugar
$^1/_4$ cup (2fl oz/60ml) water
oil for deep-frying
CARAMEL SAUCE
2 tablespoons grated palm sugar or brown sugar
1 can 5oz (150g) coconut cream
$^1/_2$ teaspoon rice flour or cornstarch
2 teaspoons water

Make caramel sauce first: Gently heat sugar in small saucepan until melted. Add coconut cream and stir until sugar is dissolved. Combine rice flour and water and stir into saucepan; stir until sauce boils. Keep warm while cooking bananas.

Cut bananas into quarters. Combine palm sugar and coconut and roll banana pieces in mixture, pressing firmly to coat.

Heat oil at a moderate temperature in deep saucepan. Combine rice flour, sesame seeds and sugar in bowl. Gradually whisk in water to form batter. Dip banana pieces into batter and deep-fry until lightly browned on all sides. Drain well on paper towels.

Serve banana pieces hot with warm caramel sauce.

SERVES 4

Citrus and Ginger Fruit

This ever popular fruit salad is simple to make. The citrus flavors really add zing and the salad is refreshing on a hot summer's day. The fruit mixtrue can also be served with Coconut Ice Cream (page 146).

1 mango
$^1/_2$ small pineapple, chopped
2 kiwifruit, chopped
1 banana, chopped
pulp of 3 passion fruit
2 teaspoons grated lime zest
1 teaspoon grated lemon zest
2 tablespoons lime juice
1 tablespoon lemon juice
1 tablespoon sugar
1in (2.5cm) piece fresh ginger, finely shredded
1 tablespoon liqueur such as Grand Marnier
  or Malibu

Combine fruit in bowl and mix well. Combine zests, juices and sugar in small saucepan and stir over very low heat until sugar is dissolved. Stir in ginger and liqueur. Pour mixture over fruit and mix well. Let stand 2 hours before serving to allow flavors to develop.

SERVES 4

VARIATIONS

- Use fresh seasonal strawberries and raspberries in place of pineapple.
- Toss in a handful of halved coconut macaroons just before serving.
- Add 3 tablespoons shredded fresh mint.

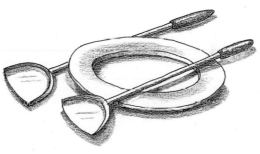

Sticky Rice Dessert with Ginger Syrup

Sticky, or glutinous, rice is very popular with the Vietnamese and is often made into a dessert. I've added Asian pear—chop the pear just before serving.

1/2 cup (4oz/125g) glutinous rice
3/4 cup (6fl oz/185ml) water
3 tablespoons dried split yellow mung beans
2 teaspoons sugar
1 tablespoon coconut cream
1/4 cup (1 1/2oz/45g) brown sugar
1 tablespoon water
3/4in (2cm) piece fresh ginger, peeled and thinly sliced
1 small Asian pear, chopped
1/2 cup (4fl oz/125ml) coconut cream

Place rice in small bowl with enough cold water to cover. Let stand overnight. Drain, rinse and drain well. Bring 3/4 cup water to boil in heavy medium saucepan. Add rice and mung beans and return to boil; boil 1 minute. Pour off as much water as possible and return pan to very low heat. Cook covered, 20 minutes. Remove from heat and let stand 10 minutes before removing lid. Add sugar and 1 tablespoon coconut cream and toss with fork.

While rice is cooking, prepare ginger syrup. Combine brown sugar and 1 tablespoon water in small saucepan and stir over low heat until sugar is dissolved. Add ginger and simmer uncovered about 2 minutes or until syrup is thick.

Using large ice cream scoop or spoon, scoop rice mixture onto 4 dessert plates. Sprinkle pear around rice. Drizzle with ginger syrup, arranging some sliced ginger on rice.

Serve dessert warm, passing remaining coconut cream separately.

SERVES 4

Tropical Fruit Molds with Mango Cream

These refreshing desserts make a cool finish to a hot, spicy meal. Make them up to two days ahead, keeping them in the refrigerator.

1 3/4 cups (14fl oz/435ml) water
2/3 cup (5 1/2oz/165g) sugar
1/3 cup (2 1/2fl oz/80ml) lime juice
1/4 cup (2fl oz/60ml) boiling water
1 1/2 tablespoons unflavored gelatin
18oz (565g) can figs in syrup, drained and chopped
1lb (450g) fresh red papaya, chopped
1 kiwifruit, peeled and sliced
MANGO CREAM
1 small mango, peeled and chopped
1/2 cup (4fl oz/125ml) sour cream
1/2 cup (4fl oz/125ml) coconut cream
2 teaspoons sugar

Combine water, sugar and lime juice in medium saucepan and stir over low heat until sugar is dissolved. Remove from heat.

Combine boiling water and gelatin in small bowl and stir until gelatin is dissolved. Stir into lime syrup and let cool to room temperature.

Lightly oil six 1 cup (8fl oz/250ml) molds. Pour 1 tablespoon lime syrup mixture into each mold, and refrigerate until set. Top with about 1/2 tablespoon each jackfruit and papaya. Pour enough syrup over just to cover fruit; refrigerate until set. Continue layering with remaining fruit and syrup until all are used.

While molds are setting, prepare mango cream. Mash or puree mango until smooth. Combine with sour cream, coconut cream and sugar in small bowl.

Turn molds out onto dessert plates. Serve with mango cream and sliced kiwi.

SERVES 6

LEFT: Tropical Fruit Molds with Mango Cream

Coconut and Golden Raisin Rolls

These rolls are best eaten hot out of the oven, but are also good cold. They can be made up to a day ahead.

1 envelope dry yeast
2 tablespoons sugar
¾ cup (6fl oz/185ml) warm milk
2 cups (9½oz/300g) all-purpose flour
2 tablespoons unsalted butter, chopped
½ cup (3oz/90g) chopped golden raisins
1 egg yolk, lightly beaten
1 tablespoon shredded coconut
Filling
1 cup (3oz/90g) shredded coconut
1 egg white
2 tablespoons sugar
¼ cup (2oz/60g) unsalted butter, softened
1½ tablespoons grated lime zest
Glaze
1 tablespoon sugar
1 tablespoon boiling water
1 teaspoon lime juice

Lightly grease baking sheet. Combine yeast, sugar and milk in small bowl. Cover and let stand in warm place for about 10 minutes or until frothy.

Sift flour into large bowl. Rub in butter with fingertips, then mix in raisins.

Make well in center of flour mixture. Add yeast mixture and egg yolk and mix to form soft dough. Place dough in lightly greased bowl and cover loosely with greased plastic wrap. Let stand in warm place until doubled in size, about 45 minutes.

For filling, combine coconut, egg white, sugar, butter and zest in small bowl and mix well.

For glaze, combine sugar and boiling water in small bowl and stir until sugar is dissolved. Stir in lime juice.

Knead dough on lightly floured surface until smooth and elastic, about 5 minutes. Divide dough evenly into 6 portions. Roll each portion into 6in x 10in (15cm x 25cm) rectangle. Spread coconut filling evenly over each rectangle, leaving 3/4 in (2cm) border. Roll up from one short side to form rolls. Arrange on prepared baking sheet. Cover with clean towel and let stand in warm place until well risen, about 30 minutes.

Bake rolls in 400°F (200°C) oven 8 minutes. Reduce heat to 350°F (180°C), cover rolls with foil if overbrowning and bake 20 more minutes or until rolls are well risen and sound hollow when tapped. Turn out onto wire rack and brush hot rolls with glaze. Sprinkle with shredded coconut.

MAKES 6 ROLLS

Sesame Almond Cookies

These great-tasting cookies can be found at Vietnamese bakeries—about three times the size of these.

6 tablespoons unsalted butter
⅔ cup (5½oz/165g) sugar
1 teaspoon grated mandarin or orange zest
1 tablespoon sesame seed paste (tahini)
1 egg
¾ cup (3½oz/110g) all-purpose flour
½ cup (2oz/60g) ground almonds
2 tablespoons sesame seeds, toasted

Cream butter, sugar and mandarin zest in bowl until just combined. Add sesame seed paste and egg and mix well.

Stir in sifted flour and almonds in 2 batches to form soft dough that comes away from sides of bowl. Wrap dough in plastic wrap and refrigerate 30 minutes.

Roll level tablespoons of dough into balls and roll in sesame seeds. Arrange 1½in (4cm) apart on lightly greased baking sheet. Flatten slightly.

Bake in 350°F (180°C) oven until browned, about 12 minutes. Let stand 3 minutes, then loosen with metal spatula. Let cool on baking sheets.

MAKES ABOUT 20

Crusty Pineapple and Cashew Tartlets

These tartlets have a beautiful crisp pastry that melts in the mouth. Be careful when lifting them out of the pans. If you like the taste of ginger, add 1 teaspoon of grated fresh ginger to the coconut cream mixture.

½ cup (2½oz/75g) all-purpose flour
½ cup (2½oz/75g) self-rising flour
1 tablespoon plus 2 teaspoons powdered sugar
6 tablespoons unsalted butter, chopped
1 egg yolk, lightly beaten
1 tablespoon water, approximately
2 tablespoons coconut cream
1 egg, lightly beaten
1½ rings glacé pineapple, finely chopped
¼ cup (about 1oz/35g) roasted unsalted cashews, chopped

Lightly grease 12-hole shallow round-based tartlet pan.

Sift flours into bowl. Stir in 1 tablespoon powdered sugar and rub in butter. Add egg yolk and enough water to make the dough cling together. Gently knead into ball. Cover dough with plastic wrap and refrigerate 30 minutes.

Divide dough evenly into 12 portions. Roll out each portion on lightly floured surface ⅛in (3mm) thickness. Cut into rounds using a 2¾in (7cm) fluted cutter.

Place each round into tartlet pan and lightly prick bottom with fork. Bake in 400°F (200°C) oven until lightly browned, about 5 minutes. Cool.

Mix remaining powdered sugar, coconut cream and egg in small bowl. Divide among tartlet shells. Sprinkle with pineapple and cashews.

Bake tartlets in 400°F (200°C) oven for about 10 minutes or until set. Let cool in pan.

MAKES 12

Banana and Pistachio Crescents

These delicate little crescents are not typically Vietnamese but do contain such ingredients as pistachio nuts, bananas and rice wine or rum, which give them a Vietnamese flavor.

1 cup (5oz/150g) all-purpose flour
6 tablespoons unsalted butter, chopped
1 tablespoon powdered sugar
1½ tablespoons water, approximately
1 egg yolk, lightly beaten
2 teaspoons finely chopped pistachio nuts
FILLING
2½ tablespoons shelled pistachio nuts, finely chopped
2 small bananas, finely chopped
1 teaspoon honey
1 teaspoon rice wine or rum (optional)

Sift flour into bowl and rub in butter. Add powdered sugar and mix well. Stir in enough water to make mixture cling together and to form soft dough. Cover with plastic wrap and refrigerate 1 hour.

For filling, combine pistachios, bananas, honey and rice wine in bowl and mix well.

Divide dough in half. Roll out each half to ⅛in (3mm) thickness. Cut into rounds using a 2¾in (7cm) fluted cutter.

Spoon level teaspoon of filling onto center of each round. Brush edges lightly with water, then fold pastry over to enclose filling. Press firmly to seal edges. Arrange crescents on greased baking sheet. Brush with egg yolk and sprinkle with chopped pistachios.

Bake in 375°F (190°C) oven until lightly browned and crisp, about 10 minutes. Let stand 3 minutes, then loosen with metal spatula. Serve warm or cold.

MAKES ABOUT 20

Banana and Coconut Tart

This tart can be kept for a couple of days in the refrigerator. It is quite simple to make and has a delicious banana and coconut flavor.

1 unbaked 8in (20cm) deep-dish pie shell
1 cup (8fl oz/250ml) coconut milk
1/4 cup (1 1/2oz/50g) grated palm sugar or
   1/4 cup (2oz/60g) brown sugar
1/4 cup (2fl oz/60ml) coconut cream
2 eggs, lightly beaten
1 teaspoon grated fresh ginger
3 small bananas, chopped

Line pie shell with parchment paper; fill with dried beans, rice or pie weights. Bake in 400°F (200°C) oven 10 minutes. Remove paper and beans and bake pastry 8 more minutes. Reduce oven temperature to 350°F (180°C).

Combine half of coconut milk with palm sugar in saucepan and stir over low heat until sugar is dissolved. Combine mixture with remaining coconut milk, coconut cream, eggs and ginger in bowl and mix well. Line bottom of pastry with bananas. Carefully pour coconut milk mixture over. Bake until knife inserted in center comes out clean, about 40 minutes. Serve tart warm or cold.

SERVES 6

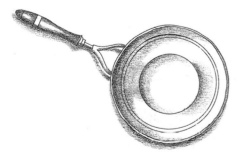

LEFT: Banana and Coconut Tart

Coconut Pancakes with Mango and Passion Fruit

Use a tropical liqueur such as Malibu or, if you prefer, an orange-flavored liqueur. The pancakes can be made several hours ahead and reheated just prior to serving.

1 cup (5oz/150g) self-rising flour
1/4 cup (2/3oz/20g) coconut, toasted
2 tablespoons sugar
1 egg
3/4 cup (6fl oz/185ml) milk, approximately
2 tablespoons shredded coconut, toasted
MANGO AND PASSION FRUIT
1 large ripe mango, peeled and seeded
2 tablespoons liqueur
pulp of 4 passion fruit

Sift flour into bowl and stir in coconut and sugar. Lightly beat egg and milk together. Gradually add to flour mixture, mixing to form smooth, thick batter (you may need a little extra milk). Let stand 30 minutes.

Heat greased frying pan, add 2–3 tablespoons batter and cook until bubbles appear on surface. Turn pancake and cook until puffed and lightly browned underneath. Repeat with remaining batter, keeping pancakes warm if it is close to serving time.

For fruit mixture, chop mango. Puree half of mango in blender with liqueur until smooth. Stir in passion fruit pulp.

Serve hot pancakes drizzled with mango puree and topped with remaining chopped mango and shredded coconut.

SERVES 4

VARIATION
In place of milk, use coconut milk for stronger coconut flavor.

The Essentials

Red Curry Paste

4 cloves garlic, crushed
1 small onion, chopped
3 tablespoons chopped lemongrass
2 tablespoons chopped fresh coriander
8 red chilies, chopped
2 teaspoons galangal powder
1 teaspoon shrimp paste
1 tablespoon paprika
$^1/_4$ cup (2fl oz/60ml) oil
1 teaspoon ground coriander
1 teaspoon ground cumin

Combine all ingredients in food processor and grind to paste.

MAKES ABOUT $^3/_4$ CUP (6FL OZ/185ML)

Chili Oil

$^1/_2$ cup (4fl oz/125ml) oil, preferably peanut
5 red chilies, chopped

Heat oil in small saucepan until hot. Remove from heat and add chilies, being careful mixture does not bubble over. Let stand at room temperature until cool. Strain into glass jar or small bottle and seal well. Store for up to a month.

MAKES $^1/_2$ CUP (4FL OZ/125ML)

Chili Lime Sauce

8 red or green chilies
4 cloves garlic, finely chopped
$^2/_3$ cup (5$^1/_2$fl oz/160ml) lime juice
2 tablespoons fish sauce
2 tablespoons chopped fresh coriander

Combine all ingredients in food processor and grind to paste.

MAKES ABOUT 1 CUP (8FL OZ/250ML)

Green Curry Paste

10 small green chilies, chopped
6 green onions, chopped
4 cloves garlic, crushed
3 tablespoons chopped lemongrass
$^1/_4$ cup (2fl oz/60ml) oil
$^1/_2$ cup ($^1/_2$oz/15g) chopped fresh coriander
2 teaspoons shrimp paste
1 teaspoon grated lime zest
$^1/_2$ teaspoon ground cumin
$^1/_2$ teaspoon ground coriander

Combine all ingredients in food processor and grind to paste.

MAKES ABOUT 1 CUP (8FL OZ/250ML)

Chili and Peanut Sauce

$^1/_4$ cup (2$^1/_2$oz/75g) sugar
$^1/_3$ cup (2$^1/_2$fl oz/80ml) white vinegar
2 red chilies, chopped
1 tablespoon chopped unsalted roasted peanuts
2 green onions, finely chopped

Combine sugar and vinegar in small nonaluminum saucepan and stir over low heat until sugar is dissolved. Add remaining ingredients and let cool.

MAKES ABOUT $^1/_2$ CUP (4FL OZ/125ML)

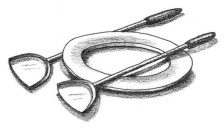

ABOVE: *Clockwise from top right: Red Curry Paste; Chili and Peanut Sauce; Chili Lime Sauce*

Peanut Sauce

2 teaspoons oil
2 cloves garlic, crushed
1/2 teaspoon grated fresh ginger
2 teaspoons sweet chili sauce
1 tablespoon hoisin sauce
1/3 cup (2 1/2fl oz/80ml) water
1 1/2 tablespoons smooth peanut butter

Heat oil in small saucepan. Add garlic and ginger and stir over medium heat about 2 minutes or until aromatic. Add sweet chili sauce, hoisin sauce, water and peanut butter and stir until smooth. Let cool.

Make sauce up to 1 week ahead and store, covered, in refrigerator. If sauce becomes too thick on standing, thin with a little water.

MAKES ABOUT 1/2 CUP (4FL OZ/125ML)

Fish Dipping Sauce

1 1/2 tablespoons boiling water
1 tablespoon sugar
1 small red chili, seeded and finely chopped

2 cloves garlic, crushed
1 tablespoon rice vinegar
1 1/2 tablespoons lime juice
1 1/2 tablespoons fish sauce

Combine water and sugar in small bowl and stir until sugar is dissolved. Let cool.

Add chili, garlic, vinegar, lime juice and fish sauce to the sugar syrup and mix well.

MAKES ABOUT 1/2 CUP (4FL OZ/125ML)

Scallion Oil

1/3 cup (2 1/2fl oz/80ml) oil, preferably peanut
3 green onions, finely chopped

Heat oil in small saucepan until hot; remove from heat. Add green onion, being careful mixture doesn't bubble over. Let stand until cool.

Strain oil into glass jar or small bottle and seal well. Store up to a month.

MAKES 1/3 CUP (2 1/2FL OZ/80ML)

Glossary

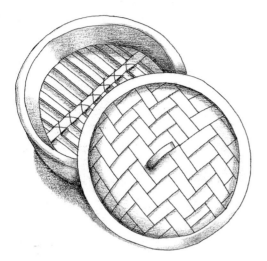

Bamboo Skewers

Available in different lengths from supermarkets and Asian food stores. Soak them in water for an hour or so before using; this helps keep them from burning. They are commonly used in Thai cooking for satés.

Bamboo Steamer

Available in different sizes. Choose one about 10in (25cm) diameter, with a lid. Place the steamer into a wok one-quarter filled with boiling water. Add the food to be steamed and cover with the lid. Keep an eye on the water level in case you need to add more boiling water. You can use a saucepan steamer (stainless steel is best) if you do not have a bamboo steamer. You can also buy a steaming tray for your wok that fits into the wok above the base; the wok will need a lid to keep the steam in. You will find bamboo steamers, steamer trays and wok lids in Asian grocery stores.

Cleaver

Choose a cleaver that feels comfortable in your hand. It should be well made and very sharp. It can be used for chopping anything from whole uncooked chicken to vegetables. It is best to use a cleaver on a wooden board. You will find cleavers in Asian grocery stores.

Julienne

Fine sticks of an ingredient, usually vegetables. Typically about 2in (5cm) in length. Cut the vegetable into lengths or pieces, then into thin slices lengthwise, finally into thin sticks. Julienned vegetables require only a short cooking time.

Kitchen Scissors/Poultry Shears

Use good quality scissors that will cut through small poultry bones. They can be used for many things, from cutting cooked chicken in half to cutting paper for lining baking pans.

Parchment Paper

A high-quality cooking paper with a nonstick coating that eliminates the need for greasing. Available at supermarkets and cookware shops.

Ribbed-Grill Pan

A heavy cast iron pan, coated with a black surface. It has raised lines along the bottom that leave the distinctive charred lines across cooked food. Grease the pan and heat until smoking before adding food.

Roasted Nuts

To roast, spread raw unsalted nuts over baking sheet. Roast in 350°F (180°C) oven about 5 minutes or until nuts turn light golden brown. Remove from baking sheet to cool.

Stir-Fry

The term used when frying food quickly in a wok. Not a lot of oil is used and the quick stirring and turning of the food prevents it from burning or sticking. The best utensil for stirring is a round-edged wide spatula-spoon. If you don't have one, use a large metal spoon or wooden spoon. The oil is heated until very hot before the food is added. When stir-frying meats, it is best to fry a handful at a time. This prevents the meat from stewing in its own juices.

Toasted Seeds

The quickest way to toast seeds such as sesame is to stir them in a dry heavy frying pan over medium heat until they become light golden brown. Remove from pan to cool and stop browning process.

Woks

Are found in a variety of sizes, metals and finishes. Traditional woks are round-based and made from thin iron or steel. Choose one that is about 14in (35cm) in diameter. Before using a new traditional wok, scrub it well. Brush liberally with oil, then heat for 5 minutes. Wipe out the wok and repeat the oiling and heating process twice more. Wipe the wok out thoroughly then it is ready to use. Don't scrub the wok after using; just wash with hot soapy water.

GUIDE TO MEASURES

As the enjoyment of good homemade food and the love of cooking spreads throughout the world, it's important to have easy-to-follow conversion of measures in our recipes. In some countries they use metric measures, in others imperial measures, and many cooks like to use handy cup and spoon measures.

- ◆ The metric measuring cup holds 250ml
- ◆ The metric measuring tablespoon holds 15ml
- ◆ The metric measuring teaspoon holds 5ml

The conversions given in the recipes in this book are approximate. Any differences amount to only a teaspoon or a tablespoon, which will not make a noticeable difference in these dishes.

Note: Imperial differs from American only in that 1 imperial pint = 20oz, not 16oz.

Dry Measures		Liquid Measures		Helpful Measures	
US CUSTOMARY	METRIC	US CUSTOMARY	METRIC	US CUSTOMARY	METRIC
½ oz	15g	1 fluid oz	30ml	⅛ in	3mm
1oz	30g	2 fluid oz	60ml	¼ in	6mm
2oz	60g	3 fluid oz	100ml	½ in	1cm
3oz	90g	4 fluid oz	125ml	¾ in	2cm
3½ oz	100g	5 fluid oz	150ml	1in	2.5cm
4oz (¼ lb)	125g	6 fluid oz	185ml	2in	5cm
5oz	155g	8 fluid oz	250ml	2½ in	6cm
6oz	185g	10 fluid oz	300ml	3in	8cm
6½ oz	200g	16 fluid oz	500ml	4in	10cm
7oz	220g	24 fluid oz	750ml	5in	13cm
8oz (½ lb)	250g	32 fluid oz	1000ml	6in	15cm
9oz	280g		(1 litre)	7in	18cm
10oz	315g			8in	20cm
11oz	345g			9in	23cm
12oz (¾ lb)	375g			10in	25cm
13oz	410g			11in	28cm
14oz	440g			12in (1ft)	30cm
15oz	470g				
16oz (1lb)	500g				
24oz (1½ lb)	750g				
32oz (2lb)	1kg				

Oven Temperatures			
These oven temperatures are only a guide. Always check the manufacturer's manual.			
	C (CELSIUS)	F (FAHRENHEIT)	GAS MARK
Very slow	120	250	1
Slow	150	300	2
Moderately slow	160	325	3
Moderate	180	350	4
Moderately hot	190	375	5
Hot	200	400	6
Very hot	230	450	7

Index